Economic Inalienable Sovereign Rights of Peoples

by
Raymond M. Carreau

WHITMORE PUBLISHING COMPANY
Ardmore, Pennsylvania

ISBN 87426-041-8
Printed in the United States of America

This work in socioeconomics
is dedicated to the memory of
my late grandfather, E. L. Williamson.

To Vegas Hinrichs
From
Your Friend,
Raymond M. Carreau

FEBRUARY 16, 1979

Contents

	Introduction	vii
1	Delegation of Powers	1
2	Rights, Powers, and Ownership of Sovereignty	11
3	Constitution	15
4	Liberty	25
5	Government	32
6	Self-Government	43
7	Value	55
8	Currency	64
9	Economic System	87
10	Effects	102
11	Natural Resources	130
12	Control of Production and Distribution	137
13	Summary	149

Introduction

Economics is an integral part of sociology.

The Constitution of the Government of the United States of America constitutes a more detailed contract among a people to base a format for government than is found in most other nations, and for this reason it is used generally throughout this treatise as an example and for comparative analysis with other socioeconomic systems.

Sociology, like biology, is in a constant state of evolution. Every political-sociological "ism" that appears on the stage of history is but a stepping-stone toward a socioeconomic golden age for humanity somewhere far in the future. It can be said that every new world concept in sociology contains within itself the seed of illogic that brings about its eventual destruction by a newer, more logical concept, all experimental stepping-stones toward an eventual golden age.

Political ideologies are changed only by internal revolutions and external wars, never by voting. The argument can be put forward that the National Socialist Workers' Party in Germany changed the nation's political ideology in 1933 by a free, open election. This is only partly true. Adolph Hitler was a fairly well-known army war hero whose new political party gained effective political control of the army and extensive influence in the navy. Failure to have allowed his party representation participation at the polls in 1933 would have brought about a revolution. So, in effect, it was still force that brought about a change of political ideology.

Once a national sociology or world-concept sociology group gains political control of a nation, it generally divides its ideology into two or more "name" political parties. This gives the political illiterates of a nation the impression that they have a choice of ideologies, where, in reality, they have only a choice of political personalities controlled within the framework of one ideology. This system makes it difficult for a new ideology with limited access to publicity to plant effective roots in a nation, because the emotions of the people vacillate between the heavily publicized name parties where they erroneously believe they can find a change of ideology. These name parties develop minor differences in time, but the basic ideology remains the same. The politicians who become prominent in the name parties have been carefully prescreened by the controllers of the propaganda of the nation to assure the controllers that their political puppets are and will remain docile supporters of the established ideology. An old truism in politics is: who controls the propaganda of a nation controls the administration of government, because with the control of propaganda you make the politicians and break the politicians. A politician who deviates from the established ideology finds himself faced with a nationwide propaganda campaign waged against him to drive him out of his seat of political influence. He has then three choices: adjust quickly and make amends to the controllers, retire from the political arena, or found a new political party so appealing to the mass of citizenry that mass organizing takes place more rapidly than the controllers of government can utilize existing laws through police force and military force to destroy the new political movement.

The nations badly need an economic system that will keep the labor force and natural resources of nations in a constant harmonious relationship. As we view the various degrees of capitalism and socialism utilized by governments throughout the world, we witness only experiments in socioeconomics toward a more logical future. The main problem that prevents more rapid progress in sociology is the people who can be classified as *dogmatists.* In the main they are people of average intellect who, when they adopt an idea—however illogical—and they are in varying degrees products of illogical cultural heritages, fanatically resist change. To these people, change is always viewed as dangerous radicalism and evil.

Mental laziness and lack of mental depth are the norms for most people. Possibly one person in ten thousand has the mental ability to adapt quickly to a more logical political ideology change; and it is from this small percentage of the population of the world—people who are not mentally addicted to an illogical historical cultural heritage—that are found the leaders for socioeconomic change.

The Creator or Creation gave one lamp, and only one lamp, to illuminate our torturous path on this world and eventually the entire universe: the lamp is called *logic.* When we conduct our affairs in a logical manner, the forces of the universe, controlled by the Creator or Creation or whatever, are benign toward us. When we are illogical, the universe frowns and we suffer, depending on the degree of lack of logic in our affairs—socioeconomic or technical.

Mainly, people are mentally and emotionally addicted to their cultural heritages, which are in large part illogical. Therefore, conflict between peoples is inevitable; and so the great task of people is to determine logic and be guided accordingly.

Viewing the United States of America form of constitutional government, the people have their authority in the Constitution by use of bylaws. This question arises: then why cannot these bylaws be drawn in such manner as would permit the people of that nation to be governed by the terms and conditions of their contract, rather than as subjects to laws enacted at the discretion of the Congress of the American government?

Since the contract exists between the members of a sovereign people, in order to arrive at a clear concept of a method by which the Constitution of the United States of America could be viewed as a contract, in which the signatories of same could be governed by its terms and conditions, logical analytical reasoning is required in the sciences of government and economics.

To attempt to reduce the rights of the members of a sovereign people through organization for government by use of a constitution contract to a systematical or concrete state and whereby the members are governed by the terms and conditions thereof, one is confronted, as in mathematics, with the problem of postulating certain principles as bases for reasoning and by which regulations or bylaws may be enacted, based upon said principles, and coordinated to form a system. Otherwise one is left in the position, as in the present political procedure of the American government, of merely expressing an opinion on matters political without the use of coordinated data for proof of same.

It follows in sequence that the administration of constitutional government, because of the lack of these coordinated data, must be made through the use of inflexible laws enacted at the discretion of a government congress. Although certain rights of the members of society have been stated in generalities, in the form of reservations in the American Constitution, the reserved rights are subject to revision due to changing conditions of a free economy and more especially by the adoption of new principles such as the American labor and cooperative laws, making same a part of the people's economy, and thereby changing the free economy to a restricted economy. This, in turn, effects the former interpretation of these generalized rights of members of society, relative to the powers of the Congress, and without the formality of changing the Constitution.

The word *postulate,* as used herein, means an essential preliminary, an assumed fundamental, a principle, a basis for a starting point; and it is therefore the postulate of the present interpretation of the American Constitution that people should discard it as not being sound and substitute other postulates as bases for political procedure.

Because of the apparent misunderstanding of the importance in which the private ownership of property and a monetary system are involved in any economy, the following treatise is presented with postulates assumed and the reasoning therefrom, to enlighten people on the limitations of powers which may be delegated to a governmental body by a sovereign people by means of a constitution, in which the personnel of the contracting members thereof, as a body, is ever changing.

In the final analysis it is the people that must decide on the soundness of the postulated theory of value as given herein and also on their inalienable sovereignty. It is to societies throughout the world that this treatise is submitted in order that a comparison may be made with the postulated theory of the present interpretation of the Constitution of the United States of America, as an example, wherein sovereignty is vested in the agency of government. Therefore by reason of the present interpretation, the equity rights in the ownership of the public domain of the living generation and its posterity do not exist. If it is the decision of societies that sovereignty, with all its implications, cannot be conferred upon an agency of government, then societies will be forced to admit that the present political procedure emanating from the present interpretation of the American Constitution and all similar constitution contract based governments is unsound.

The following treatise presents a more logical interpretation of values, and, as such, a new world concept in economics.

1

Delegation of Powers

Viewing the many and varied problems confronting the people of the United States of America, affecting the economy of the nation and the social status of its members, one is filled with doubt as to the extent of man's wisdom to meet and solve these problems. The reason for this doubt is based upon the accepting by the citizenry of the interpretation that has been made of the power delegated to their government by the Constitution as valid.

The history of past civilizations clearly indicates that the leaders of political thought, when dealing with the problems of less complex societies than those that exist today, were powerless to prevent a collapse of the governmental structures once the ownership of property, under private ownership, became too maladjusted relative to the members of the societies as a whole.

The problems affecting the economy of the United States of America have reached a state of problem complexity that dwarfs the combined economic problems of all former civilizations. This can have but one reason, because it is a certainty that the people have not advanced to a more logical form of economics because of not having introduced any new principle in their governmental procedure.

Viewing retrospectively the interpretation made by the Congress of the United States of America of the powers delegated it by the Constitution, also the sustenance of such interpretation by the courts, one is impelled by the force of logic to question such interpretation as having been made on the grounds of expediency rather than on the basis of equality of the rights of the members of society.

Doubtless, such expedience was due to lack of knowledge of procedure under constitutional government, as there was no precedent for government by written agreement of the people. It is therefore not surprising that with such written authority the American Congress should assume itself endowed with full plenary power and ownership of sovereignty and proceed to organize itself in accordance with known methods of parliamentary government. Under such assumption it deemed itself qualified, by virtue of its interpretation of its delegated powers, to regulate the value of money in a manner of its own choosing.

In this the American Congress followed the parliamentary government of Great Britain as a precedent, not having considered the fact that the Congress is only an agent of the sovereign owners of the land and all that it contains.

Since the doctrine of "all men are created equal" was introduced as an inspiration for thought and encouragement to seek separation from the parent nation, Great Britain, in order that government might be established on this principle, American society has thus far failed to achieve this ideal. At the time of adopting the Constitution as authority for government, perhaps the ambition to create a state in which equality of rights stood as the prime factor was too early in its setting. But whatever the reason, the people have now arrived at a condition in which it is of paramount importance that they review the conclusions of their predecessors relative to the rights of the people and also the powers of the American Congress delegated to it by the Constitution.

As a natural compliment to their system of private ownership, the American people have reached out and harnessed energies of nature. These energies are without and have no claim on goods or a voice in government, yet are made to labor and produce goods of every description in competition with human energy. Energies of nature are quite unlike units of human energy, which have a claim on both goods and a voice in government. Yet in a robot sense they are units of energy contributing to production, and the value of such labor is necessarily added to human energy labor in balancing value in currencies' relationship to commodities.

Economic philosophies of private ownership with corresponding inflexible laws enacted at the discretion of the American Congress and with a declared value in the units of the American people's money offer no solution as to the method by which money can be kept in circulation. With the constantly increasing span of human life and the constantly increasing population and a limited volume in the monetary system, American society is faced with the problem of keeping the units of money in circulation.

The complex condition of the American society is the direct result of their method of organization. It is, therefore, logical to inquire into it. Does the interpretation made of the powers of the American Congress delegated to it by the Constitution follow in logical sequence to the origin of power under a constitution of a people, wherein its contracting membership consists of an ever-changing personnel? Since this question involves both sovereign and private ownership of land in perpetuity, then the following problems are entitled to a careful analysis. What is sovereign ownership? Where did it originate? Who holds sovereign ownership? What relation does it bear to private ownership? What is the relation of private ownership to money? How does the regulation of the value of money affect private ownership? How does it affect sovereign ownership?

People deciding to institute a form of government of a kind and nature that will permit said society, dividing itself into myriads of subdivisions of labor, and instituting a system of private ownership of defined units of land, and distributing the products of land and labor by the use of a monetary system, and retaining the liberty of sovereignty unto itself, encounter logical fundamentals involved in a venture of this nature that must be understood.

Society, when organizing itself in accordance with the foregoing provisions, must first establish for itself the facilities through which it must work in order to avoid establishing a dictatorial power to cause a division of the product of labor. These facilities are composed of two factors: the private ownership of geographically defined units of land, and a monetary system.

Before these facilities can be caused to function in a manner that will equitably serve society, it has four exceedingly important problems to decide for itself.

First, shall each member of society have equality of expression when entering into a contract in which an agency for government is instituted and endowed with the necessary plenary and regulatory power to enforce the terms of the contract? And, if so, upon what qualifications shall such equality be established?

Second, where the rights, powers, and ownership of sovereignty are permanently entailed to society, as an ever-changing body, can the agency for government, thus created, and as in effect the executive head of a corporate body, be endowed with discretionary power over the civil liberties of the members thereof? If not, upon what basis shall the limitation of plenary power be set, as distinguished from regulatory or corporate power?

Third, upon what ground must the power of the congress be limited by society in the regulation of the value of money and for what purpose must money be regulated, when dealing in their ownership of equities under the authority of a continuous contract in which the signatories to it, as a body, are ever changing, and in which all of society even into the future own corporate equities?

Fourth, what are the conditions that must be imposed upon the private owners of land and what are the values that can be used as distinguished from utility values, as a basis for the regulation of the value of money?

The regulatory laws enacted and which control the manner of governing the private ownership of property and the monetary system constitute the economic system necessary to govern a society; otherwise they must be governed by dictatorial laws.

The fundamentals involved in each of the foregoing four problems have been interpreted by the American Congress and said interpretation has been sustained by the courts of the United States of America in a manner that is proving to be wholly inadequate and erroneous. It is the purpose of this treatise to call to the attention of the American people the ambiguities involved in said interpretation.

To arrive at the following fundamentals certain conclusions that have always been regarded as final, therefore indisputable, were, after studying the facts of human relationships appertaining thereto, found to be in error. As proof of the foregoing statement the following facts are submitted.

First, the accepted conclusion of the equality of people under the law as the qualification for the equality of their creation, is challenged on the ground that it does not settle the first question. Since the contract was, theoretically, entered into by all of society before the agency of government was in existence, then what standard for equality must be recognized to create government? Therefore, to accept this conclusion one must admit of the sovereignty of government over people's civil rights to enact their laws in a manner of its own discretion. This reasoning must be denied because of the fact that such power cannot be conferred upon their government, when they are governed by a continuous contract in which sovereignty has been permanently entailed unto themselves in order to extend the franchise of liberty of sovereignty to posterity. Therefore, by authority of their constitution, their inalienable sovereignty is substituted as the qualification for people's equality of creation.

Second, the authority of their agency of government to grant title to geographically defined units of land in perpetuity as an absolute ownership, subject only to that of eminent domain which is the right of the State, is denied. The denial of such power is based upon their inalienable sovereign ownership, as a society, of all land—and that each is an equity holder therein; and that title to geographically defined units of land in perpetuity can be given to members of society only as a conditional ownership, subject to the corporate equity rights of all living members of society in the products thereof.

Third, the power of the government to declare the value in the units of money is denied because said declaration does not provide the people with any method by which they can regulate to members of society the benefits of their corporate equity, and by which they can bring the values of labor and the products of labor into balance by regulation. Said declaration is an infringement upon the people's sovereignty because it denies to them the right to circulate their money as a labor credit measurement, which, in turn, would permit the balancing of the values of labor and its products, also by reason of the conditions imposed upon society when circulating money with a declared value, by use of property debit in private contracts (borrowing). People's sovereign rights can not be abridged or restricted except and only in their contract relations. They can not be abridged by a discretionary power of the congress.

Fourth, all presently known economic philosophies and theories of political science are discarded on the grounds that all such are based upon the definition of the word *value*, by combining all values under one definition—as an abstract thing, together with the accepted interpretation, in status quo, of the delegation of the powers of the American Congress contained in the people's Constitution, as not being correct. Therefore by substituting a breakdown in values, and having therefrom use of labor and the products of labor, would distinguish such as exchange values apart from utility values and permit people to legislate in such manner that the values of labor and the products of labor are the consequence of a common antecedent, wherein they differ from the antecedents of utility values.

By so doing people are then enabled to establish the units of their monetary system as credit for labor measurement and circulate same by use of a blanket debit over all production, giving the people a monetary system unlimited in its volume. This in substitution for the present limited monetary system which must have the constant stimulation of credit created through private, corporate, and government, and its subdivisions' contracts, such as notes, mortgages, and bonds, to keep the people's limited monies in circulation.

Although the following questions are phrased as leading in their implications, and are given for the purpose of clarifying to the American people their rights and limitations, the power of the government and its limitations, relative to the Constitution of the United States, they are also of the greatest importance to the society of every country that has achieved a state of development that will enable them, by reason of their knowledge of their inalienable sovereignty to institute the economic system of the sovereign people as their authority for government, thereby abolishing autocratic government.

Government, by use of the *economic system,* is government by use of the principle, people's inalienable sovereignty. As such there can be no division of opinion for the reason that a principle is a fundamental—an accepted truth. This fact precludes any possibility of having a choice in an economic system, because there is but one logical system.

Its use as the factor in permitting a division of labor, thence into myriads of subdivisions, and governing a system of production and distribution of goods through the use of a monetary system, is so infinitely greater in its potentialities to cause a reasonably equitable distribution of the products of land and labor to all members of society under any conditions. More so than are laws enacted at the discretion of legislative bodies, and in which such laws do not recognize that society is sovereign over government, that such method of government can no longer serve any useful purpose in the modern technological age and should therefore be discarded as obsolete.

In drafting a Constitution for the United States of America, did not the committee proceed from the premise of recognizing the authority of the people of the United States? In recognizing their authority, is not this recognizing their sovereignty?

Did they not proceed from the theory that all men are created equal in their sovereignty?

Is not the Constitution of the United States a contract, and if so, who are the signatories to it?

In drafting the contract was not provision made for an agency to be selected by the signatories and endowed with the necessary powers to carry out and enforce the terms of the contract?

Can the agency of government created as the executive head of the people's corporation be deemed a corporate body, separate and apart from society and therefore a party to their contract?

Is not the Constitution of the United States a continuous contract and in effect make every child, when born, a signatory to it?

Are not the signatories to the contract an ever-changing body in personnel?

Can the signatories living at any given time sign away in perpetuity the sovereign rights of the people to come?

Under such a contract is there any manner or method by which the agency for government can be made sovereign over the people in their civil rights?

Are not the people's so-called civil rights their sovereign rights?

Does the instituting of a system of private ownership of

geographically defined units of land interfere with the people's sovereign ownership of said land?

As sovereign owners of all land, are not all living members of society, at any given time, equity holders therein?

In instituting a monetary system for the purpose of making possible for each member of society to receive the benefits of his sovereign equity, can the agency instituted to carry out the terms of the contract be given a sovereign power to declare the value in the units of money?

Can the units of said monetary system be circulated against a specified debt, and if not, in what manner can money be circulated?

Have the people the power to force the agency of government to recognize the distinction between the exchange values of labor, and the products of labor from utility values, and circulate money as credit for labor?

Is there a distinction to be made between laws enacted under a plenary power from the laws enacted under a regulatory power?

Where people have retained sovereignty unto themselves, can a government congress be given discretionary power to institute regulatory laws of its own choosing?

Should not the regulation of the value of money be made the terms and conditions between private owners of geographically defined units of land in perpetuity and the sovereign owners thereof?

Can the sovereign ownership of all land be divorced from sovereign rights, and the ownership thereof be conferred on the agency of government, and if so, by what authority can it be done?

By what means can posterity be bound by such act? Is not the answer to the last question the use of the police power of the state, and if so, is not this dictatorial government?

Did the American people not start from the premise of

the people's inalienable sovereignty, and did not their Congress immediately start using discretionary power over the people by declaring the value in money, thereby preventing the people from circulating money as credit for labor?

Is the people's right to vote a privilege extended to them by their agency of government or is it their sovereign right?

To those who find it difficult to answer the foregoing questions, in accordance with this brief summary, the following analysis will show the logic from which the answers are derived.

2

Rights, Powers, and Ownership of Sovereignty

> *The person or body in which is vested the supreme or highest power in a State; the person or body having independent and supreme authority. Thus in a republic as the United States, sovereignty is in the body of enfranchised citizens.**

In defining the word *sovereign*, restriction of definition is made relative to its use as affecting the political activities of society.

The body of enfranchised citizens of the United States, having independent and supreme authority, is the sovereign owner of all land and the products therefrom, within the public domain.

Sovereign ownership, insofar as the people of the United States are concerned, relative to the land contained therein, originated in the surrender of Lord Cornwallis and his army to General Washington on the date of October 19, 1781. By this act the British government, in effect, surrendered sovereignty to all land contained within the original thirteen colonies, including the Northwest Territory, to the people of the American colonies. Other territory has since been acquired by purchase, by conquest, and by discovery.

To the individuals, their sovereign ownership consists of an undivided equity in all lands and the products therefrom

---

**Webster's International Dictionary*, 1913, s.v. "sovereign," "sovereignty."

within the public domain, and like their franchise of citizenship, it is limited to their life cycle.

Unlike private ownership of geographically defined units of land in perpetuity, equities of sovereign ownership revert to the body politic upon the holder's demise and are neither transferable nor subject to entailment.

Sovereign ownership, relative to humanity, is well stated in that immortal document—the American Declaration of Independence—wherein is stated:

> We hold these truths to be self evident, that all men are created equal, that they are endowed by their Creator with certain inalienable rights, that among these are life, liberty, and the pursuit of happiness.

Contrary to the popular conception, nothing herein is said of the physical or mental state of one's birth or development. If, as stated, all men are created equal, then in logical sequence thereof there must be a certain qualification necessary to this attainment. Such can be recognized only as being the God-given right of all men to an equal ownership of the surface of this planet for their sustenance.

Search wheresoever or as one may, nowhere will one find authority for a superior right to others to sovereign ownership of any portion of land. All men are created equal in their rights and ownership of sovereignty. They have, therefore, through organization, the sovereign right to contract and to be governed by the terms and conditions of said contract, thereby making such their inalienable sovereignty.

In the philosophy of government it seems unreasonable—in the extreme—to disregard the origin of power and substitute therefore the right to govern by the "divine right of kings."

Societies throughout the world are fast approaching a state in which they can no longer afford to be governed by laws enacted at the discretion of legislative bodies that disregard the rights, powers, and equities of sovereign ownership of the land by the members of the societies that authorized the creation of the legislative bodies.

If society through organization has the power to create legislative, administrative, and judicial offices, it has the power to direct the course of legislation toward any given objective.

In permitting the courts to decide upon the validity of so-called regulatory laws passed by the American Congress, a practical demonstration has been given by the courts of their inability to construe a contract continuous in nature, such as the Constitution of the United States.

In the validation of such legislation the birthright of every citizen has been taken from him. Their agency of government has apparently proceeded on the theory that the sovereign ownership of the land by the people does not exist and that the government has the authority to institute the laws necessary for self-government by the people and that the kind of self-government to be used by society is within the prerogative of the Congress to be determined at its discretion.

Once the usurpation of power is permitted to be interjected into a system of coordinated laws, that system is destroyed, and the usurpation of more power must be resorted to without end until sooner or later the people are governed entirely by autocratic inflexible laws. A government congress can no more establish an economic system by use of such laws, containing penalizing clauses and directed against all members of society, than it can cause any given chemical reaction by use of such laws or cause a change in speed and direction of the earth in its orbit. Government by use of such laws is government by police power.

Laws or edicts are declared by legislative bodies for producing effects within the body politic. When they are so declared at the discretion of said legislative bodies as entities unto themselves, the effects produced thereby are various.

As the industrial and trade relations of the members of

society grow in their complexity, the course of these effects becomes unpredictable. New laws are then declared to curb said effects, which in turn produce other unpredictable effects, necessitating other laws that produce other effects—and so on.

Under such a method of laws the people of all countries have and are compelled to use the factors of their economy as best they can, while their governments have steadfastly refused to enact the necessary regulatory laws that would make their factors a system. To do so would produce very important effects—effects of such magnitude as to revolutionize all existing forms of government. For the American people the authority for change is already embodied in their Constitution.

3

Constitution

The mode of organization of a social group. The constitution of a society is the organization of its individual members into specialized associations for achieving various social ends; the fundamental organic law or principles of government of a nation, state, society or other organized body of men, embodied in written documents or implied in the institutions and customs of the country or society; also a written instrument embodying rules and principles for the conduct of affairs. The Constitution of the United States of America belongs to what are often called rigid constitutions and can not be modified in its express terms, except through such processes as the Constitution itself ordains. *

Thus the nature of the Constitution of the United States, resulting through the organization of the members of society, in which have been laid down the rules and principles for the conduct of affairs, is essentially that of a contract in which the principals of such are the people. Provision is made and the procedure prescribed by which the personnel are chosen to institute the principles and to make the necessary laws under which said principles and rules shall operate. The agency for government thus created and endowed with the necessary powers to enforce the contract cannot in any sense be deemed a principal in the contract with the corporate body that created it.

The personnel of the governing body created by it have not the power of succession, but are elected to office by the

---

**Webster's International Dictionary*, 1913, s.v. "constitution."

principals of the contract at stated intervals of time.

The Constitution divides said governing body into three divisons, the administrative, the legislative, and the judiciary branches, and prescribes the powers and duties of each. It denies to each body the use of power not delegated to it. It is from this last statement that members of society, to a great degree, reserve their corporate rights. It does not confer plenary power on the Congress over civil liberties but limits its powers in this respect to that of regulation only.

This brief statement of the origin and delegation of power contained in the American Constitution is given only as a prelude to a discussion of the interpretation made by the Congress of its delegated power, also the legislation enacted under such interpretation and the sustenance of same by the courts. Since these are the laws administered by the executive heads of the American people's governmental agency at various periods of time since its beginning, then it follows that their economy established thereby, and the economic conditions of their society resulting therefrom, are the direct results of such laws.

To produce other effects in their economic conditions it is necessary to change their economic method. To change such it is necessary to change the causative laws. To change the causative laws it is necessary to examine their contract to find authority wherein legislation may be enacted of such nature that will permit of a change in said economy. By discarding the precedent of the British parliamentary government and proceeding on the theory of corporate government makes the authority for such readily discernible.

One can be confident in the fact that if such authority is contained in their contract, then the present causative laws are not in conformity with it, because such laws proceed from an entirely different fundamental, which is the antithesis of a contract of such nature as the Constitution of the United States of America.

To confirm the present causative laws one must

necessarily take the position that the American Congress is a party to the contract and endowed with plenary power over the other principals to it and is, therefore, the full sovereign owner of the land of the United States.

To assume this premise one must admit that the Constitution is not a continuous contract by the people, or else one must take the position that the generation existing at the time of its adoption was possessed with a superior sovereignty that enabled them to bind all future generations out of their sovereign ownership of all land in favor of the Congress. If such were the case, the Constitution would be deemed a dead document insofar as people's civil liberties are concerned, not withstanding the fact that they are, to a certain extent, enumerated therein.

Possibly the greatest error on the part of the members of a society is to be lulled into the belief that they are the government. Such teaching has been practiced by those in political power and others ever since the inauguration of government in the United States and is based upon the right reserved by the American society to elect public servants by vote of the people

This, they are told, constitutes their sovereign rights. With no one to challenge the limitations thus set, and in light of the decisions of their courts in sustaining the laws enacted by their Congress under its interpretation of its own delegated powers, the members of society have, by their silence on the subject of sovereignty, acquiesced to such teaching.

This, however, follows the tradition of all people of every nation within recorded history the theory that the state is sovereign over the individual; societies, by false teaching, have been held steadfast to this view.

The American State, by authority of the Constitution, is a governing body of a corporation endowed with certain plenary and regulatory or corporate powers. The personnel of the administrative and the legislative bodies are dependent upon their abilities, their characters, and their records, as their qualifications for succession to office. By consent of the sovereign people they have used and are using sovereign power in instituting their system of private ownership and the regulation of the value of money. In so doing they have disregarded the people's equities of sovereign ownership and, therefore, their corporate rights. On this basis the teaching that society is the government is absolutely false. Once the sovereign ownership is taken out of the hands of the people their liberties are then at the discretion of the State.

The American Congress, in following the precedent of British Parliamentary Government, has established a policy of government at variance with that of corporate government, thus causing members of society, in effect, to surrender their sovereign ownership of all land within the public domain to the governing body. This in spite of the fact that there is no possible way by which this can be done under a continuous contract such as the American Constitution. The reason for this is very clear: the society living at any period of time cannot bind those living at any subsequent period of time out of their sovereign ownership of the land of the nation and allocate same to private ownership, without first providing the method by which all the holders of future sovereignty could receive the benefit of their sovereign equities.

The above reasoning is in conformity with that of Blackstone, the eminent British authority on the construction of British law, who said: "Acts of Parliament derogatory from the power of subsequent Parliaments bind not." In the consideration of this statement one should not overlook the fact that in Great Britain the House of Lords holds all rights, powers, and ownership of sovereignty, and by virtue of such power, may bind the people of Great Britain by any act not encroaching upon the rights granted the people in the Bill of Rights, but may not bind any future House of Lords in any respect. Therefore, the holders of sovereignty sitting at any given time cannot bind any subsequent House of Lords.

The reasoning is equally sound when applied to the actions of the holders of rights, powers, and ownership of sovereignty in the United States. In granting title to geographically defined units of land in perpetuity, the agency of government, at the beginning of government, was encroaching upon the rights of the people of the future in their sovereign ownership, by not recognizing the corporate equity rights of members of society and taking these equities into consideration when regulating the value of money.

The source of British law is in an autocratic head having discretionary power over its subjects, even into the future.

The American people's courts, in sustaining the legislation thus enacted, seem not to have considered the Constitution as a continuous contract, the very nature of which precluded any possibility of the society living at any instant of time from entailing to its agency discretionary power over the society of the future.

In following said precedent the American people's Congress and courts have introduced and made effective in the United States the economy of the monarchical form of government, which issues from plenary power of the holders of sovereignty therein. Therefore they have had imposed upon them the same form of self-government that exists in Great Britain. Also, they have been deprived of the economy that issues from a contract or corporate form of government, with only regulatory or corporate power delegated to their agency, by which to govern themselves in the voluntary division of labor and in the production and distribution of commodities.

Sound government in which the principle that all men are created equal is recognized can be founded only on the theory that the living generation is the sovereign owner of all land within the public domain and that its membership has the right, through organization, to contract and to institute, under said contract, a system of private ownership to defined units of land in perpetuity. It also has the right to state the conditions of private land ownership and to enforce the conditions by use of corporate power delegated to its agency and to cause said agency to create the necessary laws to this end, without depriving subsequent society of the benefits of their sovereign ownership. *This fateful problem is probably the greatest one confronting society, because the destiny of government of the future will be determined in accordance with the manner of its solution.*

The Constitution of the United States is unique in the sense that it is a continuous contract, having no time limitation, and that in effect it makes every child at birth a signatory to it and therefore an equity holder in sovereignty, making him through organization a corporate equity holder. It is unique also in the respect that it is the first document in history wherein the powers delegated the agency of government and the limitation of such powers—also the rights of the people and the limitation of their rights—are clearly stated in printed form. The rights reserved by the members of society exist partly by enumeration and partly by implication. The agency of government is endowed with plenary power over what may be described as establishment of criminal law; but it is limited to the enactment of regulatory laws only relative to people's civil liberties.

The common practice by the American Congress of applying penalty to individuals for violation of laws of its enactment (both criminal and civil) has made it exceedingly difficult to differentiate between criminal and civil law or to determine if Congress was acting by virtue of its plenary or by its regulatory power. The line of demarcation between these two forms of power has never been established by the courts. Yet, the nature of the people's contract places definite limitation on the Congress in its use of either.

Assuming a hypothetical condition, one may obtain an insight on the limitation of plenary power delegated by the people to the Congress and the difference between the two forms of power: plenary and regulatory. Let us assume a condition of man in his most primitive form, where everything done by him is right because of his might and because there is no standard existing by which any act could be declared wrong. He would, under such conditions, be free to lay claim to anything that suited his fancy and be perfectly right in taking possession of it.

In the primitive man's loneliness he begins to seek companionship of others of his specie. To have such companionship he has to learn to agree not to kill his clan neighbors and not to take their women. He has to surrender these former assumed rights. As his associations grow in number, all are forced by nature of companionship in association to surrender more of their former assumed rights, thereby establishing standards of social behavior. As man progresses in his social life, penalty is applied to force recognition of these surrendered rights. The violation of any surrendered right becomes a wrong.

Thus, gradually, the basis of criminal law was formulated. It is the enforcement of surrendered rights over which agency of government has been granted plenary power.

In the same process of social evolution, man reserved to himself the right to freedom of action in matters not encroaching upon the rights of others. It is in these matters that the basis of regulatory laws are rooted.

Laws that issue from a government congress under the guise of regulatory laws, with attached penalizing clauses, are, in essence, criminal laws. Government by such is full autocratic government.

Regulatory laws consist of a set of coordinated laws for the attainment of a common objective. The objective sought by the people of the United States is a form of self-government by use of the economic system. Such laws control the use of the material factors of said system in a manner that the system should control the individual members, and the penalizing clauses should be unnecessary.

Since the postulates assumed in the following treatise interpretation are the direct opposite from that assumed in the past and present-day interpretation of the American Constitution, it follows that in order for one to grasp the reasoning from these bases, one should discharge from one's mind, temporarily, most former theories and practices of government.

Especially is this true in the issuance and regulation of the value of money; the kind and conditions of title granted to defined units of land to private ownership in perpetuity; and the relation of the individual to the state.

Since the government constitution of the American people is a contract existing between the members of a sovereign people, a body whose members are ever changing in its personnel, it is indeed difficult to understand how the members of the society can be governed by the terms and conditions of a contract and at the same time be governed by inflexible laws enacted at the discretion of their government congress.

While accepting the right of a sovereign people to contract between the members thereof, and to institute a constitution wherein provision is made for an agency to be established; the personnel thereof to be selected from the members of society endowed with the necessary powers to enforce the terms of its constitution, and the right of society to ordain and establish the same as the authority for government in the United States, the interpretation made by said agency of the delegated powers contained therein has overlooked the impossibility of transferring sovereignty of the people to the agency. The agency has proceeded on the postulate that sovereignty with all of its implications, excepting the right of the members of society to vote in choosing the personnel of said agency, was in some unexplainable manner transferred to the agency, thereby establishing the monarchical principle of government in which society is governed by use of inflexible laws at the discretion of the legislative body rather than by the terms and conditions of its contract.

These inconsistencies indicate that either the Constitution of the American people is not regarded as a contract between the members of a sovereign people or that the postulate of the present interpretation is unsound. Lacking precedent for guidance in interpreting the delegated powers of the Constitution, and with no experience in government, the people of the United States have suffered those duly elected to office to make their own interpretation of said delegated powers—and have accepted same without qualification.

Since the Constitution is, in fact, a contract between the members of a sovereign people—though this fact was and is ignored in the interpretation of its delegated powers—the sovereign people of the United States in the future should correct this fundamental error. In this, the way is provided by use of the postulates of value as given herein to regulate the value of money and to circulate same in conjunction with commodities, as labor credit measurements, in lieu of the present method of circulating money as units of value. This, in turn, makes the private ownership of defined units of land subject to the equity rights of all of society. The sovereign rights of the members of society are then, by reason of organization, reduced to the status of corporate rights. It also makes all members of society truly free, subject only to the terms and conditions of their contract. By so doing, government by use of inflexible laws enacted at the discretion of legislative bodies is eliminated.

Proof that the interpretation made of the delegation of powers contained in the Constitution was not a deliberate act on the part of the Congress to thwart the ambitions of a sovereign people, or by the courts when later on they sustained the acts of the Congress relative to same, is in the fact that the postulate of value as given herein was not known to government theorists and administrators, therefore the Congress had no other recourse than to use plenary power over the value of money in order to institute a monetary system. It is this postulate of value, used in regulatory laws, that makes the Constitution a contract between the members of the sovereign people of the United States and of their posterity.

It is the use of this principle in regulatory or corporate bylaws that reduces the sovereign equity of members of society to the status of corporate equities.

It is the use of this principle in which the Congress is mandated to enact the regulatory or corporate bylaws that enable the members of society to utilize the material factors of their economy in such manner that all may receive the benefits of their corporate equities.

It is in the use of this principle in regulatory or corporate bylaws that break the bondage of labor to capital to establish all of society and its posterity as equal equity owners in a corporation embracing all land within their jurisdiction.

4

Liberty

The historical account of the migration of the people from the western European nations to the eastern border of America is replete with their purposes in venturing into an unknown land.

The fact that they were willing to endure hardships is a testimonial to their determination to seek a better life on the new continent. Some were seeking more individual freedom; all sought economic betterment. In many cases, their migration also permitted them to escape autocratic rule: political, economic, and religious. Many years were required to properly establish themselves, developing the new lands to a point where they could live in comfort.

Because of the vastness of the new lands in the western hemisphere and the rich resources contained therein being utilized by the colonists, it was inevitable that the time would arrive when the parent European nations would look with covetous eyes upon such to enrich their exchequer through the simple process of taxation.

Because of the fact that most of the North American colonies were peopled at first through migration from the British Isles, these colonies were established in the name of the crown of Great Britain: this nation claiming sovereignty over all land from Florida to Canada, bordering on the Atlantic Coast.

The respective nations of western Europe that had gained exploration and settlement footholds on the American continents recognized the possibilities of empire and dispatched emissaries to the new continents to map and establish boundaries for the different colonies.

These emissaries were also to formulate and establish governments in the newly formed colonies. Government was administered by decree of the respective European nations and without representation of the colonial peoples

The early history of the North American colonies gives a very clear perspective of the difficulties involved in administering laws emanating from distant mother countries with months of time required to communicate with each other.

The lack of representation by the colonies in the parliament of Great Britain gave rise to suspicion that their people were not receiving fair dealing in the matter of levying taxes.

Thus friction grew between the colonies and the parent nation to the extent that it culminated in open rebellion in 1775, and by the spring of 1776 the demand was made by some of the people for complete independence. By July 2, 1776 a declaration of independence had been put in writing and presented to the representatives of the different colonies, was voted upon by twelve colonies and adopted by ten (New York did not vote, Pennsylvania and Delaware cast divided ballots). The last signature was affixed to the document in 1781.

At the closing of hostilities in 1781, Great Britain surrendered sovereignty to all land contained within the thirteen colonies and included the Northwest Territories. The colonial governments of that period of time had been established under the protection of and by the authority of Great Britain. Sovereignty was not therefore surrendered to the colonial governments but to the armies of the United Colonies under Gen. George Washington.

Articles of Confederation were drawn by the representatives of the different colonies for the purpose of bringing the colonies closer together in their social and trade relations.

Since the Articles of Confederation were drawn by the

representatives of the different colonies, now designated as states, and each state felt the necessity of preserving their full sovereignty, then all acts enacted by the central government were subject to review and had to be approved by the states before same could become operative.

Thus the government of the newly formed United States of America could declare war but had no authority to raise and equip an army. It could levy a tax but had no authority to collect same. The only function it could exercise at will was to adjourn itself from day to day. This single act, not requiring the assent of more than seven states, was as one writer of that time stated, "This, apparently its only useful function, was to convince the States that they must have something better as authority for government."

The Articles of Confederation proved to be, after a short period of time, totally inadequate for a government of the United States. (Articles of Confederation: the Constitution adopted by the Continental Congress in 1777, which expired on March 4, 1789, under the provisions of the present Constitution.)

Because of the deplorable conditions existing owing to the difference in the recognized rights of the various states to levy tariffs on the products of the other states and the practice of those of one state discounting the value of the money of other states, the need for a stabilized money was apparent as well as was the need for a free flow of commerce between the states.

A studied reading of the preamble of the American Constitution should easily convince one as to the origin of power and the determination of the people to retain to themselves and their posterity the liberties that had been won by themselves by the sacrifices and hardships of warfare.

Little did they realize that the safeguards they were attempting to put forth in the Constitution to protect their liberty for themselves and their posterity would eventually be destroyed.

Because of the incomplete statements in their contract, they inadvertently left to the Congress the duty of stating the specific terms of said contract through the use of bylaws.

For the first time in the history of government the Congress of the United States of America was called upon to make an interpretation of the delegation of power contained in a contract embodying millions of people and extending this franchise of liberty to the untold millions of people yet to come as signatories to it.

Little did they realize that the contract which they had just authorized established a limitation on their power to govern themselves and their posterity.

Little was it realized that to extend the franchise of liberty to posterity, society had to retain to itself the sovereign ownership of all land within the public domain and that the institution of a system of private ownership to geographically defined units of land had to be made subject to the equity rights of sovereign ownership of every living citizen at any time—even into the future.

They apparently did not realize that the Constitution which had been ratified by the states established the people of the United States as equal stockholders in the most gigantic corporation in existence and that its membership included all living people in the United States and all people to come therein, with fully paid in capital, which consisted of all land within the public domain and of that to be acquired in the future: in principle this was ordained by "We the people of the United States."

They apparently did not know that in instituting a monetary system the potential value of the units therein must be regulated to the potential value of the unit production of all land and labor in order to complete their system of private ownership under a contract in which all living people within the nation are on an equal sovereign ownership basis. It is also apparent that after the passing of many years of government in the United States under the authority of the

Constitution that the people have not yet learned that they can not permit the Congress to regulate the value of money and ignore their equities of sovereign ownership, thereby depriving the people of their corporate rights and their franchise of liberty.

To permit the American Congress the use of such power is to permit the Congress to invalidate the people's contract and to establish the Congress as sovereign, comparable to the British parliament, and the citizens' rights are in the same relative position to the powers of the Congress as are the citizens of Great Britain—relative to the powers of the parliament.

It precludes any possibility of reasoning their contract as being a covenant between the people and forces them to reason it as a contract between the people and the agency it has established to enforce the terms of the contract.

"Liberty" is the right of the body politic to decree relative to time under contract government. Contrary to the popular conception of such, "liberty" is not only the power to grant freedom of action to individuals but also to limit, even to prohibit, certain actions. Such is the use of sovereign power, therefore "liberty" is "sovereignty."

As affecting the individual, "liberty" is the right of the individual members of society to decree relative to the terms established by the body politic and is therefore limited to the terms and conditions as set forth in their contractual relations. Thus in their contractual relations members of society have, in effect, agreed to forego their sovereign rights and reduced same to their corporate rights. This by reason of the limitations involved in organization, and by so doing, they do not relinquish their sovereign equity ownership rights.

Both of the above definitions are limited to their rights, either singly or collectively, under a contract form of government.

Because of the failure of the American people's first, and all succeeding Congresses, to comprehend the limitations of their power when construing the contract of the sovereign people, in which contract provision was made for the Congress to make the necessary rules and regulations wherein the sovereign rights of the people would be protected to themselves and their posterity, the result of their work is the people's evidence that the Congress considers itself as the legislative branch of a corporate body separate and apart from the people in contractual relations with the people.

Their corporate rights do not exist as a privilege extended them by the Congress. The Congress has no such rights to confer upon them, but rather their corporate rights should exist by reason of their contract relations. It is therefore the duty of their society to review the acts of the Congress and cause the same to set forth the specific terms of their contract, in lieu of the present mass of laws enacted by reason of having ursurped plenary power over them.

In order for the American people to fully understand their liberty and through such to attain freedom of action for the members of society, an entirely new interpretation of the delegated powers contained in their Constitution must be made on the basis of their corporate rights. And since their sovereignty includes their sovereign ownership of all land, then the interpretation of the delegated powers of their Constitution must proceed on the theory that equities of their corporate ownership shall not be overlooked when instituting a system of private ownership of land, the product of which is distributed to all of society through the use of a monetary system, and that their corporate rights shall be held inviolate from any act of the Congress.

Under a constitutional form of government, "liberty" in the abstract is analogous to sovereignty and without limitation.

"Liberty," in the concrete, is analogous to freedom and is limited only by the terms of contract.

As "liberty" in the concrete is to members of society, so is it to states or nations in their contractual relations.

It is impossible for a people of any society to organize themselves for any purpose whatsoever—be it social, political, or otherwise—without restricting their liberty of sovereignty to a concrete or restricted state of liberty. Their liberty, then, is limited to and by their method or terms of organization.

Viewing the Constitution of the United States of America as the articles of incorporation of "we the people," then their corporate rights are analogous to their exceedingly poorly defined civil liberties of the present interpretation. It removes the necessity of having their corporate rights contested in the courts at every act of the Congress and makes the same easily understood by society, because the only limitations are those imposed in the regulation of the value of money.

5

Government

In the organization of government there has, apparently, been far too little attention paid to the origin of power and to the limitation of conferring powers involved in a continuous contract. The custom is, and always has been, that once any form of contract has been adopted as authority for government, those selected to enforce said contract have, in looking backward at other governments, adopted precedents that in all cases are based upon ruling a society by use of police power.

The fact that the personnel of the governing body is elected to office at stated intervals of time has no bearing whatsoever upon the subject.

Any society that permits its legislative body, whether said legislative body is composed of one or a multiple of men, to establish its economy at the discretion of said legislative body is permitting itself to be governed by use of the police power of the state.

Laws carry on into the future, but the personnel of society is constantly changing; therefore the police power used at the discretion of the state is governing the oncoming generations of signatories to the contract without their consent.

Many of the signatories are destined to live their life cycle with only a meager livelihood during their productive years and retire in poverty in their old age, despite the fact that they are in contractual relations with the balance of society on an equal sovereign ownership basis. With this prospect confronting many of the oncoming generations, can it be justly claimed that the American Congress has successfully enacted the bylaws of the Constitution of a sovereign people in a manner that will insure to all the benefits of their corporate equities? Rather, are they not governed by use of the police power of the state? Let us follow through to find and understand the answer.

In organization for government it is easy for one to understand the natural limitations imposed by the method used to obtain an objective when one understands the distinction between the opposites.

The first is the government in which private ownership of land, commercial industry, and a monetary governing system do not exist; the society exists in a purely communistic state.

The second is a society governed by a monetary system. If society chooses to govern itself by use of a monetary system as an aid in distributing the products of land and labor, they are faced with another set of opposites.

In the first, communist government owns all land and the products thereof. Labor is paid by the government in its performance by use of commodity tickets, redeemable in commodities in which the rate of exchange is set by the government.

In this method, the commodity-ticket money is not exchangeable between the members of society for large scale labor use or most commodities; therefore they can not circulate money as the American people understand the circulation of money.

In the second of these opposites a circulating monetary system exists in conjunction with private ownership of land.

In this method of government it is necessary to have the monetary system established in a manner that the units thereof can be used as a unit measure and a medium of exchange of private ownership.

In reasoning this method of government, we are again faced with two opposites.

In the first, the agency of government coins the money and declares the value in units thereof, making standard units of commodity for the measurement of value and the medium of exchange.

In the second, government coins the money and establishes the necessary rules and regulations whereby selected groups of society are compelled to declare the credit rate of labor in commodities in terms of money, making money the unit measure of credit for labor and the medium of exchange.

In the first of these opposites it is necessary to reason the value of money as fixed or positive by reason of the power vested in the government, in order to complete a method of private ownership of units of land as an absolute ownership.

In the second of these, money is used to express relative credit values, and by reason of sovereign ownership of all land being retained by the people, private ownership of land can be granted only as a conditional ownership and be made by use of regulatory laws in the regulation of the value of money, subject to the equity rights of all members of society.

At this point it should be made clear that there are many economic methods of private ownership administered by reason of laws enacted at the discretion of government with declared value in the units of their money; *but there is only one economic system the use of which permits the use of self-government by society, by reason of having no fixed value in the units of their money, thus permitting them to use the units of money to express the credit value of labor and the credit value of the products of labor by use of regulatory laws.*

Other than government existing by reason of having been seized by force of arms and established as dictatorial in nature, it may be said that all governments issue from contracts.

These contracts are but two kinds.

First of these contracts is that form whereby the people

of any society enter into an agreement with an individual or a small group, as an agency, wherein the people are one of the contracting parties and the agency is the other contracting party. In this form of contract the personnel of the agency may consist of one person or a body of people, having full rights, powers, and ownership of sovereignty conferred upon it by the people. By reason of this the agency is given full plenary power to govern society in a manner of its own choosing.

Second of these contracts is that form whereby the people of any society enter into an agreement between themselves wherein they retain unto themselves all rights, powers, and ownership of sovereignty, and by authority of said contract, provision is made for an agency to be selected and instituted with such powers as are necessary to carry out the terms of the contract.

The reason for these contracts to be limited to two kinds is that there is no intermediary place between the people and their agency wherein the rights, powers, and ownership of sovereignty may be vested.

It then follows that the conferred powers of the agency of government emanating from the people, the source of all political power, cannot be construed in the latter contract in the same light as the construction that has been made of the former.

Experience has shown that every attempt to merge these two principles into one contract results eventually in the gradual abandonment of the principle of the latter contract in favor of the former contract. The reason for this, so far as government in the United States is concerned, are factors that were unknown at the time of the interpretation of the Constitution of the delegation of power and which have entered into the American economy and which same factors are incompatible with the interpretation made by the Congress and sustained by the courts.

Power cannot be extended to an agency of government

except and only when the members of society lose their corresponding liberty. Liberty cannot be extended to posterity when power over same has been delegated to government.

The former contract is the basis of autocracy; and the latter contract is the basis of a corporation and is therefore, democracy.

Because of the limitation of vesting sovereignty in contracts and the fact that the same powers cannot be conferred upon an agency of government in both of these contracts, it then becomes necessary to examine both forms to find wherein they differ in principle and to determine the position of the American Constitution relative to either.

In setting forth the postulate that "all men are created equal" as an inspiration for independence, and accepting such for the right of members of society to enter into contract relations and to formulate and authorize the adoption of the Constitution as the authority for government, it becomes exceedingly difficult to understand the logic of the courts in sustaining the acts of the Congress in the enactment of laws at its discretion, governing the American people in their corporate rights. More especially is this true when said laws introduce the element of chance, a hazard, to the members of society in substitution for the benefits to them of their corporate equities.

If the members of society were acting within their sovereign rights in authorizing the Constitution as the authority for government, wherein an agency is created and endowed with the necessary powers to enforce the terms of their contract, can such an act be construed as a surrender of sovereign ownership of all land to its agency and permit said agency to confer title to defined units of land in perpetuity to private ownership as an absolute ownership, thereby denying to posterity its sovereign ownership of all land within the public domain? If so, can any person explain how such transfer of sovereign ownership can be made and enforced, except by police power of the state? And can it be explained how such police power can be conferred upon an agency when society has reserved unto itself all sovereign rights and by reason of contract has extended same to posterity?

Accepting the postulate that "all men are created equal" as stated in the American Declaration of Independence as incontrovertible leaves the American people with no other alternative than to qualify such with the superlative: all men are created equal in their rights and ownership of sovereignty.

People have visible evidence of the inequality existing in the physical or mental state of the members of society by reason of the chance of birth, which definitely eliminates birth as the qualifying factor for the equality of man's creation.

Birth as the qualifying factor for citizenship of any organized society has no bearing on equality of creation.

The discussion of the foregoing question as a subject apart from government and contained within itself would appear to be a waste of time, until it becomes apparent that its implications and its fundamental position are the basis upon which any contract for the establishment of government is founded. The conclusion reached by any society on this matter when drafting articles containing the authority for government determines whether the rights, powers, and ownership of sovereignty are reserved unto itself or whether such has been delegated irrevocably to the agency it created for government.

Since the ownership of land, as an absolute ownership over all land contained within the jurisdiction of any society, is involved in sovereignty, then the manner and kind of title that can be given to geographically defined units of land to private ownership in perpetuity is dependent upon the authority of the agency to grant such.

Where sovereignty is in the agency of government, then said agency may grant title to land to members of society in fee simple or in *allodium,* a term used to signify "without vassalage"—an estate held in absolute ownership without regarding any superior to whom duty is due on account thereof—with no paramount claim over such, excepting that of eminent domain, which is the right of state. When this method of instituting a system of private ownership is adopted, it follows that in the regulation of the value of money, the value in the units thereof must be by use of a declaratory power on the part of a legislative body, by use of a designated volume of a specified substance of great value, such as gold, or by use of credits of same, such as currencies, or both.

The theory is to make of units of money unit measurement of something of recognized intrinsic value and the medium of exchange by declatory power of government, thus completing the system of private ownership of property in which the holders of money are the owners thereof, in the same status as the holders of land. We have, therefore, on one side, units of commodities, the product of land and labor, a mass that is constantly being depleted by society and as constantly being replaced by the holders of land and contractors of labor, in exchange for units of money, a revolving fund established by society to evidence labor performed. The rate of exchange is determined by the competitive system for labor, services, property, or commodities.

The limitation of volume of money involved in the use of a monetary system of this nature makes necessary the constant creating of credit (borrowing), by private contracts—such as notes, mortgages, or bonds—in order to keep a sufficient volume of money in circulation to meet the needs for the distribution of the products of land and labor, and because of interest involved in said credits results in a very inefficient system of distribution.

In this method of instituting a system of private ownership, the American Congress has followed the precedent of all former governments and regulated the value in the units of money and has disregarded entirely the regulation of the value of the monetary system as a credit measurement to facilitate a system of distribution of money and commodities.

To disregard the value in the units of money and to regulate the value of the monetary system wherein the units are used as credit measurements for distribution of money and commodities challenges the sovereign power of every existing government to grant title to units of land in the foregoing manner, for the reason that to do so would necessarily place conditions upon the private ownership of land of such nature that recognizes the sovereign ownership of all land by the members of every society over its government, as will be shown in the following.

If all men are created equal, by the qualifying factor, in their rights, and ownership of sovereignty, it then becomes self-evident that such ownership can never be surrendered to an agency of government because of the ever-changing personnel of society. Any attempt to do so by any living generation is an attempt to impose its will upon incoming generations by use of police power of the government it has created, which act is a denial of the postulate from which the American people established government.

The history of governments, in general, is the history of man's failure to organize a society in a manner that would have permitted them to cause a division of labor through the mechanics of private ownership of land and a circulating monetary system, which would cause a reasonably equitable distribution of the products of land and labor.

The method is, and always has been, the practice of instituting the units of the monetary system as a circulating unit of value and is therefore a unit measure of value. Where credit money (currencies) are used, the same is based on a debt and used as a medium of exchange.

This despite the fact that no man has ever succeeded in giving a true and proper definition of value. Yet, government, arbitrarily, declares value in the units of money and has left it to the members of the respective societies to fight it out between themselves as best they can, to exchange their labor for the products of labor in the various divisions of their society without any manner of regulation by which the values of said labor and its products can be made to balance.

We have now reached a state in this technological age when society must take a hand in the direction of governmental affairs. No government that has ever existed within the knowledge of man is or was worthy or capable of directing the affairs of men and the destiny of government by having all rights, powers, and ownership of sovereignty conferred upon it. The time has come for change.

The alternative to this present condition would be to deprive the American Congress of the sovereign power it has usurped, because it would be impossible to confer such power upon it and retain contract government, and force the Congress to cause the American people's money to circulate as the unit measure of credit and the medium of exchange.

Once this is done, the people of the United States will have taken their third and final step in gaining true liberty and will have instituted a system of government that will endure the vicissitudes of time and will be capable of meeting all emergencies. The former contract may be likened to that of the British government; the latter contract is the authority for government in the United States.

Because of the manner in which the British government has existed since the thirteenth century, it has construed its government as being of constitutional form. This construction is derived from the three transitory steps that have been taken in protecting the rights of the people when transferring power to legislate from the king to the parliament. While a constitution, as such, does not exist in printed form, nor any part thereof, their unwritten constitution is based on precedent and tradition.

Because of the likeness that exists in the physical structure of the American government legislative bodies to that of the British parliament with no experience in contract government, it was probably only natural that the personnel of the American government's three branches assumed that they were endowed with comparable power to that of the British parliament relative to its subjects. The distinction is in the additional prohibitive clauses in the American Constitution (other than the Bill of Rights, which exists in both countries) and in the limitations involved to confer power in a continuous contract by a sovereign people who are ever changing in their personnel.

One can more readily understand the distinction existing between the Congress of the United States of America and the British parliament when a person has a clear concept of the origin of power existing in either governing body.

Following the withdrawal of the Romans from the British Islands in the fifth century, there was instituted an absolute monarchical form of government that ruled in accordance with the custom existing prior to and during that early feudal period of governing by kings or queens, bestowing lesser titles to others subservient to the crown.

Later, because of the encroachment of the crown upon what the barons considered their rights, an agreement was drawn by the barons known as the Magna Charta, and the king of England was forced to sign same in the year of 1215 at Runnymede. While the Magna Charta was drawn in the name of the people of Great Britain (England), its real purpose was to protect the power of the feudal barons. Thus this first step limited the power of the crown to legislate on certain matters affecting the rights of the people of England, and transferred this power to the parliament.

The second transitory step in reducing the power of the crown and transferring such power to the parliament was taken in the year 1689. The guarantees contained in the Magna Charta had become so disregarded by the crown that the people demanded further guarantees of their individual rights.

These rights were enumerated in the Bill of Rights, and, soon to be king and queen, William and Mary were forced to sign same as a condition of their being crowned king and queen of Great Britain, thus conferring greater legislative power upon the parliament.

The third and final step in the transferring of legislative powers to the parliament was taken in the adoption of the Acts of Settlement in the year 1700. By this act all legislative power was taken from the crown and vested in the parliament. Thus since the year 1700 the House of Lords is vested with the sovereign power to legislate relative to the restrictions of the Bill of Rights. While in the British rule of procedure, certain types of legislation, especially appropriations, must originate in the House of Commons, the sovereign power is in the House of Lords. No court of Great Britain may declare an act of the House of Lords unconstitutional.

6

Self-Government

Self-government, under a contract form of government wherein the society of such has retained sovereignty unto itself, is a form of government under regulatory laws, wherein each of the laws are coordinated in a manner that each law is implemented by the other.

Since the purpose of laws is to produce effects, then in order to regulate effects, each of these regulatory laws must of necessity be of such nature and arranged in such manner as to direct the course of said effects to a given objective.

Under the American government's present method of so-called regulation, the people have no economic system but rather an economic method. This is because of the assumed power of the Congress to declare the value in the units of money. When this assumption is accepted by society as conforming with its mandated power to the Congress, the Congress then has no other course than to enact all laws relative to this focal point. To declare the value in the units of money takes value out of the realm of regulation because of having disregarded the factor of time and therefore, in effect, becomes an attempt to fix value.

It then follows that all laws enacted by the Congress must be directed toward controlling the individual members of society with penalizing clauses for violation. To have an economic system, the regulatory laws must be directed toward controlling the factors of said system, and the system would then control the members of society.

Where the rights, powers, and ownership of sovereignty

are retained by the body politic for the purpose not only of having the advantage of this form of government for itself but also to extend this franchise of liberty of sovereignty to its posterity, then every living member of any society at any given period of time is an equity holder in the sovereign ownership of all land and the products thereof and constitutes the people's paid-up capital as shareholders in their corporation.

To insure to members of society the benefit of their corporate equity, all laws that have been enacted at the discretion of their legislative bodies which in any manner affect their trade relations and which have established their economy of private ownership as an absolute owner of property with its complement—a declared value in the units of the monetary system—must be eliminated and substitute the economic system of equities of sovereign ownership.

In this system the factors of the economy, which are private ownership of units of land as a conditional ownership and units of money without a declared value by the Congress, are regulated in a manner that both the products of land and the units of money will at all times reflect the credit value of labor performed and should insure to all of society, through regulatory laws, the benefits of their corporate equities.

In the use of regulatory laws governing a people under a contract in which all are equal in their holdings of an equity in corporate ownership, no fixed standard of value can exist; to have it so would destroy the flexibility of the regulatory laws and then each law would have to be made inflexible relative to the fixed standard, thereby denying to society the right to use money as a unit of measurement to determine the credit values of labor performed. Also, it would deny to the sovereign people their right to the use of their money in such manner that the units would, at all times, reflect the relativity of all credit values of labor to the products of labor. This will be more apparent in this treatise after a study of value and money.

Since government by use of the economic system, which is based upon equities of sovereign ownership of all land by the people, has never existed in recorded history, it is not surprising that the Congress of the United States of America could see no clear line of demarcation between the use of a plenary and a regulatory power. Many laws have been enacted by the Congress to control certain groups of society and industries under the guise of regulatory laws, but they always contain similar penalizing clauses directed toward the individuals, as are laws enacted under its plenary power.

In the consideration of regulatory laws, every American citizen should understand that he or she is a signatory to a contract of government and that the personnel of their agency, as an assumed corporate body, separate and apart from the people, is not a signatory to said contract. As individuals they are on the same basis as all other citizens.

The right to interpret the delegated powers contained in their contract is the right of every citizen.

It is also within the citizens' rights and within their power to determine for themselves, collectively, if there is a distinction to be made in laws enacted under the plenary power of Congress from those enacted under the regulatory power.

A plenary power is a full power, absolute.

A regulatory power is a limited power and in every case is limited to the subject in question.

The difference between sovereign ownership and private ownership parallels closely the latter's relation to a renter.

Sovereign ownership of property is to private ownership of property as a private owner of property is to a renter.

The granting of title to geographically defined units of land to private ownership in perpetuity does not, in any sense, interfere with one's sovereign equity of same or the products thereof, regardless of who performed the labor of production.

Sovereign equity is an undefined equity in all land and the products thereof, contained within the jurisdiction of, in this example, the United States of America.

Since, through organization, the people's sovereign equities are reduced to the status of their corporate rights or equities, then in contract government the people are dealing in equities of corporate ownership, and the regulatory laws necessary to establish the economic system are for the purpose of governing said system. And as before stated, there is but one economic system. Following this line of logical reasoning, the Congress of the United States would have no other alternative than to enact the necessary regulatory laws that will protect to all of society their sovereign equities and their corporate rights.

The very nature of contract government precludes any possibility of trading, selling, or transferring equities of corporate ownership. Such ownership cannot be dealt with through the use of the monetary system, as such ownership is intangible, undefined—except on a pro rata basis with all citizens—and limited to the owner's life cycle.

It is inconceivable that the members of an educated society, entering into contractual relations, would sign away their joint sovereign ownership of land to private ownership in perpetuity by dividing said land into geographically defined units thereof, without first protecting their sovereign equities. Neither is it conceivable that they would permit their agency of government to construe the powers delegated to it in a Constitution in such manner that said agency of government could confer title to geographically defined units of land to private ownership in perpetuity, and by so doing, deny to posterity its franchise of liberty and, in effect, deny to society the benefits of their equities of sovereign ownership and their corporate rights.

Under the American form of government it is impossible to institute the principle of private ownership of land in perpetuity without the use of the necessary regulatory laws through which the conditions of private ownership can be made to conform with the equity rights of corporate ownership in the product of the land.

Since liberty is sovereignty, then if people lose their sovereign ownership, they lose their liberty. People cannot extend the franchise of sovereignty to posterity and at the same time delegate it to a government congress.

> Democracy—Government by the people; a form of government in which the supreme power is retained by the people and exercised either directly or indirectly through a system of representation and delegated authority periodically renewed, as in a constitutional representative government, or republic. Democracy is loosely used of government in which the sovereign powers are exercised by all of the people or a large number of them, or specifically and commonly in modern use, of a representative government where there is equality of rights without hereditary or arbitrary difference in rank or privilege; and is distinguished from aristocracy.*

The foregoing definition of democracy, which is similar to that of other authorities, is a good example of the American people's inability to properly define a descriptive word embracing their method of social organization when ignoring their corporate existence.

In the application of the American people's sovereign powers, we have proceeded on the theory that their sovereign ownership is divorced from their rights and that the sovereign ownership is entailed to their governing agency.

While the nouns *democracy* and *value* are seemingly far apart in their meaning, yet one feels constrained when studying the subject matter involved, in either case, to suspect that people's inability to have properly defined the noun *value* set a limitation upon their ability to define *democracy*, since in

---

***Webster's International Dictionary*, 1913, s.v. "democracy."

both cases, in order to arrive at the true state of either, one must challenge the present concept of sovereign ownership.

Since the economic system cannot be instituted and operated without the true concept of value and its application, then a word that will fully describe said application in a method of social organization must be amenable to a definition that will follow in sequence thereof.

Therefore in the definition of democracy, the sovereign ownership of all land by the people must not be construed, by inference, as being divorced from people's sovereign power. The name must describe the method of organization. It follows then that any form of government in which the sovereign ownership of all land is not recognized as being the property of the people and in which their method of government is instituted in such manner that it will insure to each of its members the full benefits of their equity of sovereign ownership cannot justly proclaim itself a democracy.

Democracy is the science of government dealing in the relativity of human rights and ownership of all land, wherein a society has organized itself and entered into contract relations on the basis of equality of creation. Since the Constitution or contract in the United States of America is continuous in nature and makes every child at birth, in effect, an equal signatory to it, evidences their equality of creation.

Using the qualifying factor that all men are created equal in their rights and ownership of sovereignty, then the sovereignty of all living people—and of all people to come—is recognized as inalienable.

In their contract relations, in effect, all agree to forego their right to individual action as sovereign and have reduced same to the status of that existing in a corporate body. An agency of government is instituted and the personnel is chosen from the body politic and endowed with plenary power but is restricted to regulatory power only over the economy and the civil liberties of the people. This limitation of regulatory power makes the governing agency the governing head of a corporation.

Title to defined units of land in private ownership is given subject to the corporate equity rights in the products of said land to all of society. Units of money are circulated as labor credit measurements and without a declared value by the agency of government.

The potential value of units of money is determined by members of society in their rate of crediting labor performed and through the use of the corporate bylaws; the products of land and labor, when reduced to the finished unit of commodity, represent credit for labor performed, and their value is in the ratio of exchange in these two different forms of credit.

The agency of government has the police power to enforce the bylaws of the Constitution but has not the power to change them, except by consent of the people.

The term *corporation,* as used in the sense of the American people's method of organization under the Constitution of the United States of America and when their regulatory laws are instituted in such manner that their corporate rights are recognized, then becomes analogous to *democracy* and may be better understood as such.

The validity of laws can be established through a representative form of government when the limitations imposed by reason of contract are fully understood.

The difference in this form of government, distinguishing it from an aristocracy, is in the limitation of power that can be conferred upon its agency by the people, said limitation being caused by a continuous contract extending into the future and embodying all of posterity as signatories to it.

When conferring power upon an agency to legislate affecting people's trade relations and instituting a system of private ownership and money, only regulatory power, under true democracy, is possible.

The American people's agency of government has neither power to confer upon itself nor privileges to extend to the members of society. It follows that only the people can confer power upon their agency and institute themselves under a contract wherein said contract extends into posterity, and in so doing, it recognizes the sovereignty of posterity. The people have by such act limited themselves in their ability to confer only regulatory power upon the agency of government.

Sovereign ownership and sovereign power are indivisible. Once society surrenders sovereign ownership to an agency, it will gradually lose its sovereign power to said agency. Once the sovereign ownership of land is out of the people's control, they lose their sovereign power by reason of the fact that the agency of government, being endowed with both plenary and regulatory power and making no distinction in its use of either, will gradually usurp power over the sovereign ownership of land and enforce its decree relative thereto through its police power. The agency makes its own interpretation of the powers delegated to it.

Since the people are unorganized, they cannot protest the agency's interpretation of its delegated power. Experience has proven that the people would rather accept the interpretation made by the agency than try to protest as individuals.

While the Supreme Court of the United States of America is an integral part of the American people's agency of government and was instituted, among other duties, for the purpose of protecting their liberty, it has proven itself incompetent in its qualification for this trust. It is the people in their contract that extend the franchise of liberty of sovereignty to posterity and not the Congress or the Courts by the use of discretionary power.

It is "liberty" in the unlimited sense, therefore, "sovereignty" that is entailed to posterity by the American Constitution. There are none, nor can there be any, restrictions placed upon the sovereignty of posterity.

In the method adopted by the Congress of establishing an economic method for society, the laws enacted that instituted the American people's present ownership of property and the method taken to regulate the value of money are in both respects laws that extend into the future and are supposed to govern the society of today, tomorrow, next year, and on into the future.

The use of discretionary power in this respect can only be enforced by use of police power. It is not the purpose of the American agency to govern their people in their corporate rights by use of police power. Such method of government does not conform with true democracy; the use of police power is justifiable only in the enforcement of people's surrendered rights and over which the American government has been delegated plenary power. It will be seen after a study of the economic system that same is self-enforcing.

Time has worked to the advantage of the agency's usurped powers, and it is exceedingly difficult to nullify these powers after long usage.

In the American form of government, the personnel of the legislative and the administrative bodies frequently changes, but the people are never at a loss to replace said personnel. At every opportunity some members of society, convinced of their superior political wisdom, seek any public office available. They are anxious to give the people the benefit of their wisdom to carry out the processes of government. Once elected to public office, they try by any means possible to accomplish, through legislative action, a fulfillment of their promises made when seeking the office. To accomplish their purpose, no distinction is made in the kind of power conferred on the people's agency by their Constitution. The fact that a power has been conferred seems to them to be ample authority and that it is their prerogative to place their own interpretation on said authority and to proceed from their viewpoint to enact legislation of their own choosing.

Because of the authority given the Chief Executive to select the personnel of the courts, with the consent of a subjective Senate, the American people have of late years been made subject to laws that are fast taking from them their civil liberties, or corporate rights, which have never been recognized as existing either by the people or by the government.

The history of the courts leaves little, if any, doubt in the people's minds that in passing upon the constitutionality of the powers delegated to the Congress that the political convictions of the individual members were the guiding motives in their decisions. This is apparent in some of the decisions of the early courts having been reversed in later years. Thus, in the final analysis, the courts are sovereign over the people and have therefore established the people's economic policy.

If the American people recognize the right of the Congress to usurp power, which should be logically denied it, and the right of the courts to sustain and enforce the laws enacted by reason of this usurped power, then the people must admit that they have no reserved rights or liberties.

The alternative to this is to challenge, in its entirety, the interpretation that has been made by the agency of government of the powers delegated the Congress and substitute an interpretation of the people's Constitution based on the precepts of a contract, in which the people of the United States of America are the contracting members thereof and that their agency of government is not a party to said contract but is rather the governing body of their corporation.

Originally, it was left to the American people's agency of government to make up the details of their Constitution through the use of bylaws, but because of incomprehension, their first and all succeeding personnel of government have failed to recognize the sovereignty of the people and to institute their contract as a going concern of relative interests of the members of society.

Thus far, experience has shown that it is unsafe for society, as a whole, to trust their general welfare to an agency. The American agency of government has departed in its entirety from the concept of a people's contract and has never recognized society organized as a corporation.

It is not the purpose herein to deny the merits of the American government in establishing the people on a plane of living superior to that of the people of most countries. The contention is that the complex conditions of the American people's economy have now reached a state that requires action on the part of the people to institute, or cause to be instituted, the details of their contract in the form of laws in such manner that recognizes their sovereignty and to abolish all existing laws that in any manner conflict with their corporate rights.

It is now the American people's duty to finish the job started by their forebears and write into their Constitution the details of their contractual relationships as the sovereign owners of the United States, thereby taking the final step to establish themselves as a true democracy, to gain unto themselves the liberty of sovereignty, to extend this franchise to their posterity.

The American people have, in order to meet the exigency of wars, suffered their Congress to delegate their president emergency powers wherein bureaus have been established, in the name of the president, with power to issue rules and regulations having the force and effect of law. This is in spite of the fact that the last clause of Section 8 of Article 1 of the Constitution confers all such power upon the Congress: "to make all laws which shall be necessary and proper for carrying into execution the foregoing powers, and all other powers vested by this Constitution in the government of the United States, or in any department or office thereof."

In the delegation of these wartime powers to the president, Congress has also denied to the sovereign people of the United States the use of their courts for redress.

A search of the Constitution of the United States of America fails to reveal authority having been conferred upon the Congress to delegate any legislative power whatsoever or to interfere with the right of citizens to seek redress in their courts for alleged violations of so-called wartime powers.

The Constitution contains the terms of the people's contract; it is up to the American people to check closely for lack of logic in the present and past interpretation by the courts. It is the people's constitutional right and duty—to determine and to force, by collective action within their power, the inauguration of regulatory laws relative to the functioning of the economic system as a guide for self-government.

By so doing the American people would eliminate the possibility of their governmental agency making an interpretation of the power delegated it in such manner that makes said agency sovereign over the people. By inaction on this matter the people will in time eventually lose their contract. By action on this matter the people will preserve their contract to themselves and their posterity.

The system of government advocated in this treatise, in substitution for the American people's present organized and constituted government, is not related to communist government based upon Marxist theory that is the political basis of the present government of the Soviet Union.

Let us make the distinction between these two systems clear: in the political ideology of Marxist Communism, the state is sovereign over everything, including the members of society, and any rights members thereof may have are only privileges extended to them by the state; under truly democratic constitutional government, however, society is sovereign, and any powers the state may have are conferred upon it by society.

It follows, therefore, that the system advocated in this treatise is a direct opposite to Marxist Communism. People's inalienable sovereignty makes it impossible to adopt basic communist sovereign-government theories as authority for government. In the people's sovereignty, the people can view their agency for government only as an agency to serve and maintain their corporate rights.

7

Value

Value is a term used universally to denote a relationship, and the different values can be defined relative to their functional properties only, in determining any specific relationship.

In the regulation of the value of money in accordance with the regulatory laws given herein and from which it is possible to establish the economic system, the necessity of defining abstract value and how it exists in all things as a premise for reasoning the economics of private ownership is eliminated entirely.

In instituting the economics involved in sovereign ownership by the people, the premise used as a basis for determining the regulatory laws is the right to the benefits of one's equity of sovereign ownership—therefore, one's corporate rights.

It is an assured fact that if the individual is a holder of an equity in sovereignty, then all economic philosophies that have been expounded prior to this treatise on the subject, insofar as government in the United States of America is concerned, are worthless as guides for government.

To attempt to group the values of labor, services, money and commodities with rentals, interest, air, water, sunshine, sleep, or profit under one relationship and to define such in a manner that can be used universally as a guide for legislation governing a system of production and distribution of goods is futile. The reason is that said values are not the consequence of a common antecedent. It is only values common in their derivation that can be classified and defined as a group. Thus any definition of value that has ever been given and used as a premise for economic reasoning can easily be disproven by showing the difference in the antecedents of the different values.

Values are consequents, which may or may not be relative, depending upon their antecedents. As such, values in exchange by use of money exist in their potentialities and can be defined and measured only in their exchange ratios at any given time by use of relative factors.

This is exemplified in the value of food to people's bodies, which stands in an entirely different light than when used to denote the relationship of food to money.

When we speak of the functional properties of value, such as food and medicine to people's bodies, their antecedents differ from the antecedents of values that are in exchange by use of money in people's trade relations. Since their antecedents differ, all values cannot be defined in the abstract; only those relative in their antecedents can be defined in the concrete.

Thus an antecedent of all values entering into people's trade relations is *labor,* therefore, all such values can be reduced and measured as credit for labor. Since credit evidence may or should exist in two forms in people's trade relations, the *product of labor* and *units of money,* then the term *value,* as used in this sense, is the exchange ratio of the products of relative antecedents. The potentialities of credit values in both forms are used as the relative factors to express said ratio.

Value in the former case is in the molecular structure of food and medicine wherein they yield readily in the process of digestion for the nourishment of people's bodies. In this sense the utilitarian theory of value is applicable.

By reason of the limitations people impose upon themselves because of recognizing the assumed power of a government congress to declare the value of money as being valid, any who attempt to define the word *value* must confine said definition relative to the use of said assumed power.

Declaring the value in the units of money and denying to the members of society, collectively, the right to declare the redemption rate of goods in money, is in effect a declaration by the American Congress that the sovereign people of the United States of America shall not have the use of the units of their money and the commodities they produce, as evidence of their credit for labor, and that they shall not use the true concept of the relativity of values from a common antecedent as the basis for the exchange ratio of these two different forms of credit.

It is only when the American people deny the Congress the use of this sovereign power over society that they would be in a position to define and measure values by use of their relative antecedents.

It is not the purpose of the people's agency to govern them in their civil rights but rather is their duty to institute the regulatory laws necessary so that members of society may govern themselves by use of the economic system. When their agency of government usurps power, the use of which transcends the rights of the members of society, it is the right of society, as stated in the American's Declaration of Independence, "to alter or abolish the use of such power and to institute a new government, laying its foundation on such principles and organizing its power in such form, as to them, seems most likely to affect their safety and happiness."

In the regulation of the value of money for the determination of the benefits of equity holders of corporate ownership, people are confronted with a problem far different from the regulation of the value of money as a standard unit of commodity for comparison, as exists in the typical monarchical economy.

Thus people are spared the necessity of trying to give value a universal definition by using money as the unit measure of credit and the medium of exchange thereof.

By regulating the value of money in accordance with the

following regulatory laws, recognition is given the members of society's corporate ownership of equities and provides the method by which they receive the benefit of said equities, thereby establishing, in essence, the nearest practical approach to a true democracy. As before stated, this is the most fateful problem confronting society of the present and of the future.

The substance used for money is of no moment, as any of the ninety-odd elements, or any combination thereof, providing they could be physically controlled, would serve such purpose. This treatise does not deal in units of value in money because such do not exist in the theoretical sense.

Other than service or utility values, such as the value of clothing, food, medicine, etc., to people's bodies, and in regard only to exchange values, values exist only in their potentialities, and it is only when any two potentialities meet in exchange that values thereof are expressed and then only for the instant of time, as such potentialities are in their exchange ratios, the expression of their relationship or value at any given moment.

While the factor of time is given in the definition of value, it is used in a different sense than it is used in the survey of heavenly bodies, since in such a survey, motion of said bodies is constant. Its use in defining exchange values of labor and of the products of labor is in the changing methods and rates of production of goods; therefore, the labor factor is variable.

It is this postulate of value and the application of same by the use of relative factors in its creation in the regulation of the value of money that makes possible corporate government. Its use definitely reverses the established processes of government and makes a government congress the executive board of a corporate body, thereby establishing society as sovereign, and provides the method by which the members thereof may receive the benefits of their corporate equities in the distribution of money and commodities.

To understand how the relative factors of the exchange ratio are established by law, in the regulation of the value of money, in a manner that will bring the value of labor to balance with the value of the products of labor, see Chapter 9, "Economic System."

The illogical economic conditions under which the people of all nations are living can be traced directly to the limitation of trying to legislate under present economic theories.

In trying to solve economic problems, one may study the philosophies propounded by political economists of the past and present on the subject and find that they have set their own limitations in trying to establish a system that could cause an equal flow of goods and monies and would keep labor employed under all conditions. These limitations are, of necessity, caused by the premise they assumed in reasoning from their definitions of the word *value.*

The premise assumed by Karl Marx is, in essence, identical with the premise assumed in the Adam Smith philosophy as set forth in his book *The Wealth of Nations.*

In their attempt to define the word *value,* both Smith and Marx attempted to reduce abstract value to an entity. Both of them used the same factors, and each arrived at the same fallacious conclusion. Then they went in opposite directions in writing general philosophy.

On the part of Marx this explains, because of his inability to reason an essentially self-regulating monetary system which would keep labor employed under all conditions owing to the effects of said system, what caused him to substitute the use of dictatorial power of the government in lieu of the current competitive system based on the so-called law of supply and demand.

Adam Smith, in his *Wealth of Nations,* defines value by stating that values are created by land, labor, and capital. This is a fallacy for the reason that the effect of two causes must exist in order to produce said effect. Thus, capital, things of value, must exist before land and labor can produce capital.

Compare this definition with that given by Karl Marx in Das Kapital, in which he divides value into two classes: *use value* and *surplus value.*

Of surplus values, in effect, he states that the capitalist—and in Marxist theory all employers of labor are capitalists—is one who purchases raw material and by hiring labor converts the raw material into finished units of commodities, which he then sells at a price greater than the two cost him. Marx, probably unintentionally, by this analysis was giving a definition of profit, and in so doing, he used the identical factors of the Smith definition in the creation of value. He did not realize that there is no method by which one can purchase raw material and by hiring labor convert the raw material into finished units of commodities and have therefrom a total greater than the intrinsic sum of the two.

If, as stated by Marx, the capitalist then sells the product for other capital, he is claiming that the other capital, the product of land and labor, must first exist.

Thus the factors of the Smith definition are land, labor, and capital; and of the Marx definition are raw material, labor, and capital. Since land is the source of raw material, it is of no importance which term is used as the factor in creating value; it is apparent then that both have used the same factors, thereby establishing the same fallacy as the premise for their philosophies.

The economics of sovereign ownership provides the method by which people are enabled to control both *supply* and *demand.* Although these two factors have always been regarded as being the greatest influence in establishing the price of commodities in reasoning the economics of private ownership, they have no bearing whatsoever on establishing the redemption rate of goods in money in the economics of *sovereign ownership.*

Because of the almost universal belief in the so-called

natural law of supply and demand influencing the price of goods, labor, services, or properties, the subject merits further comment in the relations of supply and demand to value.

In the philosophy propounded by the economist John Stuart Mill, his subject is premised on the definition he had given for the creation of value. Of this, he states that value is labor, and supply and demand. Here again is found the same fallacy of definition as in that of the Adam Smith and Karl Marx definitions, in that in the economics of private ownership the price of goods fluctuates with supply and demand.

Where goods increase in price because of these so-called natural factors, then people are dependent upon capital already in existence for the sale of said goods. Therefore, said capital, the product of land and labor, must exist before goods can be sold at an increased price. This definition is analogous to the Marx definition in that he used the same factors of raw material, labor, and capital. Since capital is the product of land and labor, it must exist prior to the creation of value; therefore, an effect of the two causes, land and labor, is used as a factor in its own creation.

The term *exchange ratio,* used to express value, is not original with this treatise, as this term has been used by a certain school of economists as their definition for value. Yet because of their failure to have supplied the relative factors by which the values of labor and the products of labor could be brought to balance as a basis for legislation, their definition was inadequate, and these relative factors could not be supplied without challenging the accepted powers of a government congress to declare value. Had they continued their research in this field, it may have been quite possible that they would have arrived at the economics of sovereign ownership as the solution to the world's problem of economic unstable governments.

Other definitions have been given of this controlling word *value;* the economist David Ricardo defined value as labor; one school of economists defines value as labor credit. The inadequacy of either of these two definitions is readily discernible when one is brought to realize that in said definitions both bring all values to an abstract thing in labor, wherein society has no basis by which legislation can be enacted to bring the value of labor and the product of labor to balance. This is the all important thing in any system of distribution: without a method of bringing by legislation the value of labor into balance with the value of the products of labor, true democracy cannot exist.

There are those economists who look upon the utility of anything as more closely approximating the true concept of value. Since by this concept many values exist that are not interchangeable with the many utilities existing, then this concept of value provides no method whatsoever of bringing the various values to a given standard by relative factors in which any value may be determined relative to its utility, and is therefore, beyond control of any system of legislation.

In the final analysis, it is the exchange of values in people's trade relations that this treatise is concerned with in the use of money. Therefore it is imperative to find a common denominator of all values from a common antecedent entering into people's exchange relations.

The foregoing comments on the different theories of value are given only for the purpose of showing the inadequacy of definitions as a premise for establishing a policy of government; yet there is no escape as long as, for example, the American people accept the interpretation made by their government congress in its delegation of power contained in the Weights and Measures Clause of the American Constitution as being valid.

It is fundamental that a reasoning can be no more sound than its premise; if the premise is a fallacy, then the reasoning therefrom is equally as fallacious.

Because of the lack of people's ability to define value in a manner that all values can be reduced to relative factors by use of a common denominator as a basis for legislation, they are forced to rely upon a declared standard unit of value; therefore, all legislation affecting their trade relations must of necessity be enacted relative to this arbitrarily declared value, thereby denying to members of society the existence of their sovereign ownership and the right to use their money as a crediting base for their labor.

There is no way by which the values from a common antecedent can be reduced by use of a common denominator when accepting the validity of a declared value by a government congress, because the declared value, money, must exist in the same category as all other values. The only manner in which this can be done is to circulate money as a credit for labor. By so doing, economists are spared the necessity of defining abstract value and using said definition as a basis for reducing economics to a political science. This enables people to substitute the right to the benefits of their equity of sovereign ownership as a basis for the regulation of the value of money and thereby to establish policy in government, in accordance with corporate government.

Under contract government, it is not within the power of the people to institute a sovereign government with power to regulate privileges extended to society, but rather it is within their power to institute a government endowed with the necessary power to regulate the corporate rights of a sovereign people.

8

Currency

A corporate form of government is the recognition of the sovereign ownership of all land and the products thereof by the living generation and that each member of society is an equity holder therein. Therefore, there cannot be a division of sovereignty of the people with an agency of government, by divorcing sovereign ownership from sovereign rights and powers, and retain liberty.

In this form of government, it is necessary to depart from all former theories and practices in the issuing and use and manipulations of currency and establish its use in a manner that the units thereof will reflect the relative credit values of labor and the products of labor, in contrast to the present method of reflecting abstract values.

In considering each member of society as a holder of an equity of corporate ownership of land, it should be remembered that each member is also a holder of an equity in the corporate ownership of all products of land.

Since private ownership of property and a monetary system are instituted for the purpose of permitting a division of labor among the members of society, then private ownership and money constitute the facilities through which the division of the benefit of equities of ownership is made. Money (currency) then becomes the unit measure of credit and the medium of exchange of private ownership of anything used in people's exchange relations.

To accomplish this, a complete revision of the method of issuing and the regulation of the value of money is necessary. It will take from, for instance, the Congress of the government of the United States of America the discretionary power it is now using in declaring the redemption rate of gold in terms of money. The clause contained in the American Constitution delegating to the Congress the power to coin money specifically limits the power of the Congress over the value thereof to that of regulation only, which is the direct opposite of a plenary power and which limitation retains the Constitution as a contract between the people and extends the franchise of liberty to posterity.

This does not necessarily require a change in the Constitution, as the authority for it exists in the Weights and Measures Clause in Article 1, Section 8: "Congress shall have the power to coin money, regulate the value thereof, and of foreign coin and fix the standard of weights and measures." However, in order to clear doubt as to the meaning of this clause, when considering it in conjunction with the people's inalienable sovereignty, a slight change in the wording is suggested.

In the interpretation of the delegated powers contained therein the Congress assumed and later the interpretation was unwittingly sustained by the courts that the verbs *regulate* and *fix* were synonomous and it had therefore the authority to fix value in the units of money, thereby making it a standard unit of commodity. In the foregoing assumption, the agency of government established the typical monarchical economic method of government in the United States, wherein said method does not recognize sovereign ownership of all land and the products thereof by the people.

In analyzing this Weights and Measures Clause, no fault can be found with the act of the American Congress in fixing the standard unit measure of weights and measures as being inflexible in their content, as this clause specifically authorizes such, even fixing money, as a unit of measurement, but it does not tell the Congress to fix money as the unit measure of value.

It will be noted that the first part of this clause limits the power of the Congress over the value of money to that of regulation only.

To disprove the synonomy of regulate and fix, *regulate* is a relative term and implies motion within limits, *fix* is a positive term and without regard to motion.

By reason of the Tenth Amendment to the Constitution—"the powers not delegated to the United States by the Constitution nor prohibited by it to the States, are reserved to the States, respectively, or to the people"—the right to declare the redemption rate in commodities is reserved to the people.

The states, upon becoming signatories to the Constitution, surrendered any and all rights over money in order to have a unified monetary system common to all of the states.

The assumption thus taken by the Congress as to the synonomy of regulate and fix had the effect of establishing the power of the Congress on the same plane, relative to the citizens of the United States of America, as is in the power of the parliament of Great Britain, relative to British subjects, thereby destroying any chance of contract or corporate government existing in the United States.

The Congress, when exercising the power to declare the value of money relative to gold, or anything else, is using full plenary power, while its authority was that of regulatory power only, as contained in the Weights and Measures Clause.

In order that this clause may be more fully understood and brought to conform with corporate government, a change in the wording is now necessary. In its present form, it does not specify any particular purpose for the regulation of the value of money. The wording of this clause is loosely drawn and would imply that the Congress could regulate it for any purpose at its discretion. This despite the fact that the Constitution is a contract dealing in equities.

Therefore a change in the wording of this clause to "Congress shall have the power to coin money, regulate the value thereof as a labor credit measurement" would clarify the purpose of money.

A casual reading of this necessary amendment would hardly serve to convince one of its far-reaching effects, but when a thorough study is made of it to the extent that it is fully understood in its implication, one is in a position to understand that it will:

(1) cause people to stipulate the dual nature of their credit system as existing in money and commodities;
(2) force people to get away from abstract value and separate therefrom the concrete values in which they are dealing by the use of money in their trade relations;
(3) force credit through the regulation of the value of money to be given for all labor performed, regardless of the source of energy used in performing the labor;
(4) take from the Congress all discretionary power over the value of money and force the Congress to conform with its mandated power to regulate units of money as credit measurements;
(5) take from the Congress all discretionary power over civil liberties, as all legislation must be made relative to the regulatory laws that establish the people's economy as corporate owners of all land and the products thereof;
(6) definitely end any chance of laws having to be reviewed by the courts as to their constitutionality, relative to civil liberties;
(7) change the present modified autocratic form of government to a true democratic form of government, which is, in the final analysis, corporate government in which all of an ever-changing people are equal corporate stock holders.

The potency of this clause to govern a society, when rightly construed as to its delegated power in connection with contract government, is so vast that it is beyond the power of one to grasp its limitations, if such there are.

Since in contract government we are dealing in equities of corporate ownership, then the power to declare the redemption rate of production must of necessity be vested in the people. Then it is the duty of Congress to regulate the manner in which said declaration shall be made.

The value of money is determined by the use to which it is put. Its value, as a credit measurement, is entirely different from its value as a measurement of abstract value, as is used in the monarchical monetary system. (*Monarchical monetary system* is a term used in this treatise to identify the type of economics historically associated with monarchy governments and subsequently retained by nonmonarchy governments that followed.)

In the monarchical system the value of money is established by a legislative body and issued to society to be used as a basis of comparison of values by members of society in their trade relations and wherein no rules are established for making these comparisons. A sovereign people have the right to the use of their money for the measurement and crediting of labor performed, regardless of the form of energy used in performing the labor in the production of goods. A sovereign people also have the right, that rules in the form of bylaws by the Congress shall be established, governing the method of measuring and crediting the performance of labor.

Where the power of the Congress to declare the value in money is denied and society demands that the Congress cease and desist from the usurpation of power to declare the unit value of money, then obviously people are confronted with the problem of establishing their money in such manner that units of money will reflect the relative credit value of labor and the products of labor. It is in this that the postulated theory of value is introduced and made the basis for legislation through the use of bylaws which govern people's corporate existence.

The very nature of contract government precludes any

possibility of a profit of such nature as is permitted under the monarchical system. It is doubtful if the members of an enlightened society would, in entering contract relations with fellow members of said society, consent to allow a profit to some, at the expense of themselves, when all are on an equal corporate ownership basis.

The profit system as used at present is, in effect, a private system of taxation and gives to the purveyor of commodities a decided advantage over the working classes of society who sell their labor on a daily basis.

Because of the disadvantage of the worker in bargaining for the sale of his labor, provision is not made for the tax imposed and known as profit in establishing his wage scale. When producers of commodities are able to institute machinery in the production of goods, oftentimes a machine may dispense with many workers, and no provision is made in the present sociological structure wherein said dispensed workers may have the benefit of their equity of corporate ownership, despite the fact that they have a birthright ownership equity in land, machine, electrical current used, commodities produced, etc. Under the present monetary system, the purveyors of commodities may deliberately fluctuate the monetary value of commodities, using as an excuse the so-called law of supply and demand, and tax the workers all excess monies paid to them for labor performed above their cost of living. This benefit is taken by the purveyor of commodities as profit. Can this procedure be reconciled with contract government?

It is not the purpose here to try to present arguments against a profit system but rather to follow through in logical sequence, in reasoning the principles involved in corporate government. Even under corporate government a profit system of a limited nature may be instituted, but profit must come from a source different from that which now exists.

Assuming that gold were to be used as money, units of gold would then become the labor credit value for gold, or any other commodity, the same as the credit value for labor. Its use in this respect is as a symbol of credit and bears no relation to its intrinsic value; prepared clay would serve the purpose equally as well.

Because of the fact that it has often been the custom to settle international trade balances by the use of gold, there is no logical reason why such practice should not continue, on the basis of the declared valuation of gold of other countries. Such practice would not, in any manner, interfere with the herein proposed economic system, for the reason that money would circulate without a specified debt in gold—with the exception of the labor production value of gold—therefore, gold would be of no use as a basis for values.

Other commodities could be used equally as well to adjust international trade balances. This statement undoubtedly will cause much comment, but when one considers the elimination of the profit system as it is now known and understood, then international trade balances will be extremely small, since foreign trade as a requisite to an economic system is not necessary. Foreign trade in foodstuffs and raw materials for manufacturing is desirable for people's comfort but bears no relation to an economic system.

The economic system of a corporate form of government is strictly internal, and in this respect, is unlike the economics which issues from the use of a monarchical monetary system; which system must be kept, as nearly as can be, adjusted to the economy of all other nations through the use of gold.

Since the units of the monetary system of a corporate form of government are used exclusively as labor crediting and measuring, then in the exchange of goods with people of other nations the values of their goods should be reduced to the labor crediting value of production, in which case it would be of no importance whether settlement of trade balances are in the form of money or of commodities.

The volume of money in circulation may be a moot

question, since the profits to be derived under corporate government must necessarily come from the amount of money in circulation.

The amount of profit that anyone may acquire is a problem for future society to determine.

In a monetary system instituted for the purpose of using the units thereof as the credit measurement of labor, said money cannot be circulated against a debt. Because of the free status of units of money, there appears to be no theoretical limitations on the amount that can be issued by a government or of the rate of issuance, although it is quite probable that there may be practical limitations on both the amount and rate of issuance. This question apparently is one to be determined through experience in its usage.

To circulate money as the unit measure of credit for labor destroys any possibility of circulating money as a credit for any form of capital—such as gold and silver, or securities of any nature—nor can it be circulated as a credit for property, as such would be an infringement on the rights of future sovereignty. Thus the limitation imposed by reason of corporate government forces people to circulate money as the credit for labor performed.

In the light of people's present knowledge on this point, the control of which seems most apparent on the rate and issuance of money, is the limitation of profit upon those in the manufacturing group, since it is in this group in the field of industries that the greatest amount of labor, numerically compared to the employer, exists and is the point of greatest concentration of raw materials and of the finished units of commodities.

The reason for a lack of a theoretical limitation on both the amount and rate of issuance of money is in the unit rate of crediting labor in its performance. Where commodities and money are instituted and made the basis for crediting labor, then the rate of crediting labor adopted by industries and the profits deemed necessary to stimulate private initiative are the factors that would determine the circulating volume of money.

The rate of crediting labor in its performance may be established at five dollars per hour or ten dollars per hour—the ratio of exchange of credits remains equal—but the volume of money in circulation becomes relative to the rate of crediting labor. Thus it may be found necessary for industries to adopt a standard rate of crediting of labor in order to control the volume and rate of issuance of money. On this point, societies should exercise the greatest care to avoid allowing their government congresses to declare the crediting rate of labor in order to control the volume and rate of issuance of money. To delegate such power to a government congress would have the effect of permitting the congress to declare the value of labor, thereby giving people a fixed point, which in turn would give society a dictatorial form of government.

One cannot too greatly stress the importance of this fact: that a government congress must not be permitted to fix the crediting rate of labor. To do so is to fix the value of labor, which in turn would destroy the relativity of labor to the product of labor, as expressed by the rate of crediting of either, resulting in the requirements of all legislation to be enacted relative to this fixed point, thereby destroying government by use of regulatory laws and the economic system based upon their corporate equities.

In theory, to permit a government congress to establish by law the rate of crediting labor would give people a system with the same defects as those in the present method of permitting the American Congress to declare the value in money; both disregard the changing labor rate of the unit of commodity rate of production. Either one destroys the relativity of labor to the product of labor, as expressed by the rate of crediting of either, and destroys any possible chance of proceeding on the theory of people's contractual relations in their corporate ownership.

It leaves people with no other alternative than to proceed under the regulatory laws necessary to establish the economic system of sovereign ownership.

Self-government means just what the term implies, and it is of no concern whatsoever to people's agency of government, or any branch thereof, as to the rate of crediting labor or the potentialities of their credit values. To permit a government congress the power to establish by law any fixed point affecting people's economic system effectually destroys the relativity of their rights, powers, and equities of corporate ownership.

Under this proposed system it is the industrial groups of a nation that determine the crediting rate of commodities in terms of money, and the over or under issuance of money could not either inflate or deflate the value of money as a credit measurement.

Modern technology is not founded upon illogic but is founded upon facts established by skilled technician scientists, and there is no logical reason why people should not establish by law human relationships based upon the facts of human rights.

Equal opportunity is not the equivalent of equal rights under corporate government.

Although it may be admitted that laws are made and construed on the basis of equal opportunity, yet it will be difficult indeed to convince members of society, each having an equity in sovereignty and with disparity existing because of unequal physical and mental development, or heritage of wealth, that all members of society have equal opportunity.

Should societies be made aware of their corporate rights under a contract form of government, it would be exceedingly doubtful in case of mass unemployment, regardless of the cause, to maintain a so-called free enterprise system based upon the economics of private ownership and with an uncontrolled debt monetary system.

The unemployed members of a society have the right to

demand the benefit of their corporate equities. And there are no members of society, convinced of the merits of constitutional government, who dare to deny to all of society the benefits of their equity of corporate ownership.

The challenge of physicists, engineers, and chemists to people's political way of life by having harnessed energies of nature, by using same for labor in the field of production, and by finding new methods of production and the synthesizing of materials in the field of chemistry has left the personnel of those engaged in government—and all others who presume to guide and mold opinions on matters political in an uncertain state—hardly knowing which way to turn to meet the challenge.

The efforts of physicists, engineers, and chemists have thus far been devoted to the field of production, transportation, and communications and have left it as a political matter for society to determine the manner of distribution of their results in the field of production.

In trying to meet the challenge of distribution, the trend has been to entrust to governing agencies dictatorial power, which in essence follows closely in many respects the political doctrine of extreme socialism.

The failure thus far to improve nations' systems of distribution is the direct result of people's inability to conceive of the dual state of things once they cause a division of labor and to institute a system of private ownership of defined units of land and a monetary system whereby the units thereof are used as units of measure and a medium of exchange.

The present method of treating production, distribution, and value as existing in a single state, precludes any possibility of advancement in the field of distribution: these must be viewed from the standpoint of existing in a multiple state, separate from each other.

When society causes a division of labor, without a monetary system, wherein one member produces a commodity of some nature and another member produces a different commodity, etc., under private ownership, production and distribution of same exist then in the singular state and their means of exchange is barter. When a standard unit of money is made by decree of government a unit of value, the effect is to make of said unit of money a standard unit of commodity, thereby continuing the singular state of things in people's trade relations.

The feature enabling one to understand the difference in the use of laws enacted under a plenary power, distinguishing same from laws enacted in the use of regulatory power in the establishment of controls for the enforcement of either, is that enforcement of the former is by use of police power, while the enforcement of the latter is by limitation, which in turn is enforced by revocable permits. Doubtless, it will be argued that in the final analysis police power is the control over limitations. But let us study the effects on members of society by use of the economic system of corporate ownership, or the regulation of the value of the monetary system, to find the answer.

In the economics of sovereign ownership by the people, all products of labor entering into the channels of commerce are, through the use of the regulatory laws given herein, under a blanket debit to the credit issued for labor performed; therefore, the holders of money may redeem their credit in anything at their option at the redemption rate stated by the producer.

Unlike the credits existing in the economics of private ownership, wherein value is given to credits by specified debits in private, corporate, and government contracts (such as bonds, notes, mortgages) and are therefore subject to interest, the credits for labor performed under corporate ownership by the people, being free from specified debits, in private contracts, are not subject to interest bearing.

Production and distribution and the values thereof, in the course of distribution, become dual in nature. By establishing this dual system people then have a system of distribution which can be controlled through the use of regulatory laws in a manner that all of society may receive credit for labor performed, regardless of the energy used in the driving of machinery in the performance of labor, as compensation for the benefit of their equities of corporate ownership.

Production consists of the production of goods and the credit given for labor performed. Distribution consists of the distribution of credits, the distribution of goods, and the redemption of the credits issued.

Without the production and distribution of credits, whether it is recognized by society or not, in present complex society in this machine age, people would have to resort to barter.

Society has become so accustomed to the use of the machine production of goods that the use of said machine is looked upon only as beneficial, but it is not considered that the products of machines are detrimental to the extent that it requires political action to bring the value of their products to balance with the value of the products of human labor.

The right of the employer to introduce machinery in the production of goods, thereby eliminating considerable human labor, is hailed and justified by society because of the lower costs in production, which to society means a lower price on the commodity produced.

Labor, thus eliminated, is then told to seek employment elsewhere. Since all industries proceed on the same idea, the chances for labor in other established fields are constantly lessening. It is only when new industries come into being that the workers thus eliminated can be reemployed.

It is rare that an industry of such magnitude is instituted that spin-off from its manufacturing operations creates satellite industries and services.

The best example of this is the automobile industry, because the automobile has necessitated various affiliated industries and has created an enormous need for service. The personnel in the service branch of this industry now exceeds that of the parent industry and its affiliates.

It is the right of all members of society to work for a living. As corporate owners of an equity in all land and the products thereof, they have the right to demand—and the government has the duty to bring about—a change in economic procedure in a manner that will make available to all the necessities and the comforts of life.

In an organized society, every member has the right not only to the bare necessities but to comforts people have created, because of their corporate ownership.

For many years the American people have had a very clear case of their government having authorized a pyramiding in value of a debiting base in order to gain an increase in the circulation of money as credit.

Under the present form of economics there is no limit on the part of those with political power to increase the volume of money and then later, as prices in relation to wages become more maladjusted, to accuse other members of society of reducing the value of money.

If the volume of money per capita goes up, the value thereof must go down, which is the natural sequence in dealing with a monetary system with a declared value in the units and backed by a debt—by authority of government.

It is not difficult to understand that under the profit system in the normal everyday life of the people of a nation that a certain volume of money circulating is required to meet all of their needs. These needs can be summed up under four general headings: *cost of living, taxes, interest,* and *profit.*

If the items *interest* and *profit* were eliminated in people's total circulating monetary requirements, then their needs would be proportionately downward to the volume of these two items. People would then have two items less as an excuse for the manipulations of money values.

By eliminating the debiting base of money and making the units thereof the unit measure of credit without a specified debit and by instituting the laws necessary to establish commodities, the product of labor, as credit for labor, people would then have a monetary system the units of which circulate in volume in direct proportion to the volume of credits that exist in the commodities consumed.

This proposed monetary system would be immune to manipulations and would defy all efforts to interfere or fluctuate the potential values of either money or commodities.

The distinction in profits derived from present monetary systems is that new debts have to be constantly created in myriad manners in order to create the credit in volume sufficient to circulate money and allow profit. All such credits are issued against an equal debt in private contracts; therefore, all credits existing are backed by debts. In the monetary system proposed in this treatise, since the units thereof circulate as credit for labor, regardless of the energies used in driving machinery in performing labor, then said credits are debt free from private contracts and people are not limited thereby in the circulation of money by reason of a debt existing. There appears to be no logical limitation on the circulation and issuance of money. By reason of the foregoing, all members of society through time could have an excess of credits, over and above their daily needs, to meet the cost of living.

Taxation would be a tithing of monetary credit values to be distributed throughout society for cost of government; for payments to those whose jobs have been taken over by machines, and others incapacitated for labor, as the people's benefit for their equity of corporate ownership.

To accomplish this, society must take into account in formulating its political actions labor that is performed by the use of machines.

The product of labor performed by machines must be used as a crediting base for credit values in the same manner that the products of human labor are used, thus tying all of people's credits together in a manner that no earthly power could cause an inflation of money, commodities, property, or labor, any one to the detriment of any of the others.

To gain an idea as to the volume of labor performed in the production of commodities by the use of machines utilizing electrical current, let us take a hypothetical figure of an electrical company supplying energy to the industrial users of a nation. This figure is given as 115,187,000,000 kilowatt-hours for one year.

By depreciating this amount by 25 percent as not being used in the production of goods and the maintenance of equipment but rather in advertising, display, other lighting, and sundries, we would then have approximately 86,390,000,000 kilowatt-hours. By allocating 50 percent of this balance as used in the production of labor-saving and other machinery, a net balance of 43,195,000,000 kilowatt-hours used in driving machinery for the production of commodities would be left.

Since the hypothetical total production of electrical energy for *all users* in terms of kilowatt-hours is 198,160,000,000 for the nation in one year, then the amount used in this estimate for performing labor in commodity production is approximately 22 percent thereof.

Reducing 43,195,000,000 kilowatt-hours to horsepower hours at the rate of 1 ⅓ horsepower hours per kilowatt hours equals 57,493,000,000 horsepower hours.

In reducing this amount of horsepower hours to manpower hours, the low rate of 8 manpower per horsepower hour or 10 2/3 manpower hour per kilowatt-hour is used. At this rate 43,195,000,000 kilowatt-hours equals 460,760,000,000 manpower hours.

By reducing this number of hours to manpower years of three hundred working days, eight hours per day, we have approximately 191,900,000 mechanical men producing commodities as an auxiliary to human labor, and to some extent substituting and therefore eliminating human labor.

The foregoing figures enable one to grasp the trend of interfering in present methods of distribution. The users of harnessed energies for commercial production, electrical or otherwise, utilize the resources of a nation for profit by eliminating expensive human labor, regardless of the corporate equities of these resources owned by those eliminated.

The use of the present monetary system in the United States of America prohibits the use of money and the products of labor, by society, to bring into balance the values of labor and its products and leaves the American people with no method by which a division of the benefits of corporate equities may be made in order to keep their commodity distribution method operating efficiently.

Because of the highly technical nature of the term *value,* which has resisted the ingenuity of mankind to accurately define—except that mankind has attempted to define value in the abstract sense—the definition of which is so necessary as a premise for reasoning the economics of private ownership, this treatise is spared the necessity of such when reasoning the economics of sovereign ownership by the people.

This treatise is not concerned with the foregoing method of analyzing value, because the term *the exchange rate* is suitable to this proposed economic system.

It is not important what the utility value of goods are to the individual, when reasoning the economic system, but great concern must be shown about the exchange rate of goods as the economics of equities of corporate ownership are founded on this fact.

All labor performed, whether it be human labor or machine labor, in any field whatsoever, is reduced to its credit value, existing in two forms: *money,* the standard unit measure of credit; and *commodities,* the product of labor.

The use of the proposed regulatory laws gives people a system by which the credit value of commodities is reduced to the standard unit of credit, money.

All labor performed in every field is then reduced to its money credit, value.

A monetary system founded on this principle is incapable of being caused to fluctuate in its credit value, except and relative only to any given commodity at any given time.

To illustrate, by reason of an overabundance of potatoes causing their credit value to diminish, a nation's standard unit of money could not be affected, except and only relative to potatoes, and since the nation's standard unit of credit could not be circulated against property debt, then the standard unit of credit could not artificially be fluctuated, relative to any other credit value.

The exchange rate of one commodity may, at times, be changed slightly upward, while the exchange rate of another commodity may be changed slightly downward, thereby keeping the entire average commodity exchange rate in equilibrium.

One can disregard the so-called natural law of supply and demand, because the excess production of any given commodity could not greatly fluctuate its exchange rate. In the case of excess production, said excess could not reach the market because of a commodity tax law. A commodity rate redemption law prevents the individual from declaring a lower exchange rate on same. To declare a lower exchange rate on any given commodity would require action of the entire industry dealing in that specific commodity in any given community. The ability of the individual to fluctuate the exchange rate would be controlled from his source of supply. In case he attempted to do so, he would in all probability lose his supply.

It would, in effect, eliminate the individual method of pricing of goods, which is a matter of great concern to all of society, since the pricing of goods determines the rate of crediting labor in commodity production, the only source of income to society.

By use of a monetary system based on this principle, the

credit value of anything may be expressed in terms of money or in terms of anything entering into a nation's economy and may be known to all the people at all times.

The word *price* would have an entirely different significance from that of people's present conception. It would mean the commodity redemption rate in the manufacturer's hands, and, as such, it would be determined by the members of the different enterprises handling the same commodities.

After the commodities left the manufacturer's hands, the price would be determined by competition in the wholesale and retail trade.

The word *cost* also would have a different significance, because the cost of production, transportation, and distribution of commodities are, in their final analysis, the costs of labor, and the total costs of the production of any given commodity is the total sum of the credit for all labor given for such.

It is therefore of vital concern when viewing the price of a commodity that the full credit for all labor of its production has been given; as stated before, the credit for labor is the only income of society.

While it is not within a nation's province to supervise or even to suggest the kind of a monetary system that is to be used by other nations, it would be greatly to the advantage of the people of the different nations to merge their societies in such manner as to bring as many as possible under one economic system.

To come under one economic system, which means one overall government at least in the limited economic sense, is of far greater importance, for example, to the nations of Europe, than is the preservation of their present nationalities with their divisive differences of languages and customs.

Once the people of the world adopt the economic system of sovereign ownership as a method of government, then the problems arising out of foreign exchange are reduced to a minimum.

As stated before, the economics of sovereign ownership has no limitations in its capabilities for caring for mankind.

If the people of the different nations of the world could be induced to organize themselves in the foregoing proposed manner, the complicated questions involved in present foreign exchange would be eliminated.

Monies circulating among the peoples living under different governments based on the economic system would be the credits for labor issued under the authority of each country's economic system, and international trade balance, if any, could be adjusted on the basis of commodities chosen.

Where this monetary system is used, people would have a plurality of commodities as standards of values, with their redemption rates expressed in terms of money, limited only by the number and kinds of commodities entering into their trade relations because all would have their redemption rate declared by a certain class in the industrial field under the regulatory power of a government congress, as in the United States of America, or similar regulating bodies in other nations, in accordance with the ratio of exchange of labor and the products of labor applicable in each country.

Contrast this with the present American monetary system based upon having one commodity-rate redemption declared, such as gold, by a discretionary power of the Congress, with all of its attendant evils of forcing the members of society to carry on their trade relations with a monetary system the units of which are numerically limited. And because of their constantly lodging in private ownership, the members of society are forced to constantly borrow and are taxed because of a stipulated rate of interest by the holders thereof for the use of their own money; money being a facility created to complete the system of private ownership. Also, the usurped power of the American Congress to declare the value in terms of gold gives to the Congress, either directly or indirectly, authority to deny to society the right to credit the product of labor performed by the use of machinery and prevents society from bringing into balance the values of labor and the products of labor. Because of this fundamental error, society is ever at a loss to know the extent of their civil liberties. Changing political opinions, due to the changing conditions affecting the people's economy, offer excuses for the Congress to enact new laws at its discretion. These same changing conditions influence the opinions of the courts in sustaining legislation to the extent that the American people's former concepts of their civil liberties are oftentimes thrown in reverse.

Once a metallic base, as a value determination of money, is eliminated in favor of a monetary system in which the potential value of the units is established as the credit value for labor, then the holders of units of money, under the authority of a different economy, may call for its redemption in the products of labor of a kind at the holder's discretion under the authority of the economy that issued the money.

This outstanding fact would eliminate the cause for some wars between nations which are the outgrowth of economic problems.

Since the monies operating in the economic system would not call for a redemption in any specific commodity, then people's credit for labor (money) circulating abroad could not drain from its origin country and any great portion of any kind of production. Conversely, the said origin country could not deplete the monetary value of other nations.

If, for example, the money from the United States of America were held by people in other nations, they could not call for its redemption in gold; unless the American people had a surplus of gold to sell, the American money would be redeemable in anything entering into the channels of commerce. Conversely, if other nations were to accept this type of monetary system, this would prohibit the American people from withdrawing from other nations the valuations backing their monetary systems. This fact does not imply that they are not redeemable in services, labor, or property, domestically, but they are limited to the products of labor in international trade.

Once society enters into a contract form of government, it must be prepared to accept the limitation involved in such, because a contract of this nature has no time limitation and the life cycles of the contracting members are constantly changing and overlapping, so that only a portion of its membership exists at any given time. Each member is sovereign during his life cycle, and no one can bind subsequent society from their rights of sovereignty. As previously stated, sovereignty includes the ownership of all land and the products therefrom.

With these facts confronting people, it should be clear to them that they are unable to authorize the issuance of a monetary system the units of which circulate against a debt, the reason being that the society living at any given period of time is powerless to debit the property of posterity and bind posterity to recognize said debt.

The economics of private ownership teaches people that the value in the redemption base of money, guaranteed by government, is the motivating force that causes money to circulate.

There are but two monetary systems possible in which the units circulate freely among the members of society in trade relations. First is the monetary system, which has always been used since the origin of credit money and which circulates against a specified debt; second is a credit money system, which does not circulate against a specified debt.

The base of the first system is its declared value by authority of government; the base of the second system is its credit for labor value determined by society.

Since the nature of contract government logically precludes the use of the first system, people have no other alternative than to return to the terms of their contract and issue money as the credit for labor.

The impelling motive for the circulation of money then becomes the needs and desires of the members of society in their trade relations.

The benefit of equities of sovereign ownership in the product of all labor is the impelling force that circulates money. To circulate money with a declared value in the units thereof by authority of a government congress is to govern the economy of society by use of dictatorial laws enacted at the discretion of the Congress. The history of mankind is people's proof of the hazards to the members of society incidental to the use of laws of this nature; these hazards cannot be eliminated except by abolishing the use of such laws.

To circulate money without a declared value by authority of a government congress is to govern the economy of a society by use of regulatory or corporate bylaws in which a hazard to a corporate right of any member of society cannot exist.

It is possible that many economists will protest a monetary system based on this principle as corresponding to that which they understand as fiat money. The difference here is that the unit is a unit measurement of credit and not a unit of value by fiat or decree of government.

It matters not where, how, by what, or by whom, labor either manual or mental is performed; it is all incidental to people's system of production and distribution of goods, and as such, it must be charged against such goods, even against imported commodities and paid for by the importers.

Because this is the purpose, this is the only means through which people can have a practical division of labor in a free society. To accomplish this, the units of people's money must be established as credit for labor performed and redeemable in anything of credit value at the option of the holders.

9

Economic System

The word *economy* is a descriptive word used to designate, in general, the effects of causative laws directing a system of production, transportation, and distribution of goods when the members of a society divide themselves into various divisions of labor to render reciprocal service.

This is accomplished through the use of a monetary system, the units of which are used as a unit measure of credit and the medium of exchange of labor, services, property, and commodities; also where the land is divided into units and title to the units is vested in private ownership.

The causative laws enacted by a society, affecting the private ownership of property and the regulation of the value of money, are the factors that determine the efficiency in which distribution of goods is made to the members of society.

To clarify the term *economics of private ownership* as distinguished from the term *economics of sovereign ownership*, the following explanation is given.

Economics of private ownership is based upon the private ownership of geographically defined units of land in perpetuity subject only to taxation and eminent domain; also the agency of government exercises a discretionary power to declare the value in the units of the country's monetary system making same a unit measure of value and the medium of exchange, and money is therefore a standard unit of commodity. In this manner of establishing the economic method, the private owners of land have no responsibility toward the remainder of society which grants private ownership and gives the people of a nation no method by which they can bring the values of labor and the product of labor to balance by any method of legislation.

Economics of sovereign ownership is based upon the private ownership of geographically defined units of land in perpetuity, subject to the equity rights of the sovereign owners of all products of said land; also the agency of government has the regulatory power to establish units of money and units of commodities, the product of land and labor, as credit for labor performed, thereby making units of money the unit measure of credit and the medium of exchange thereof. This fact enables people, through the use of regulatory laws, to bring the value of all labor, regardless of the type of energy used in performing labor, to balance with the value of all products of labor.

Regulatory laws, like the contracts of government, are limited to two kinds: in the first—the logic of which is doubtful—the liberties of a society are at the discretion of its government; in the second—the logic of which is sound—the authority of government is at the discretion of society.

In all forms of government wherein the agency of government exercises the power to declare the value of the units of the monetary system, such acts render impossible the treatment, theoretically, of value in any other manner than as a positive thing, therefore, as an entity in itself.

In establishing money as the unit measure of value, thereby forcing members of society to make a comparison of everything entering into their trade relations to the fixed standard unit of value, the unit of money becomes the standard unit of commodity.

Although it has always been the common practice of teaching that money is the unit measure, it is not a measure in the sense that people use any other form of measurement. Value, being intangible and undefinable, as an abstract thing, can neither be measured by volume nor as a unit of force (as in the pull of gravity) nor can it be used as a standard for comparison (as a color standard); but in the potentiality of exchange values of labor and the products of labor, credit values of the product of labor can be arrived at by the use of their antecedents and measured by money.

Units of the present monetary system, for example, in the United States of America, are used as standards for comparison, and no rules are established for making such comparison. Any two people are free to make this comparison in a manner of their own choosing. This is termed the *competitive system.* Such procedure can result only in an economic method in which many of society are rewarded with a profit limited only by their ingenuity in their trade relations.

In the economic system of equities of sovereign ownership, money has no fixed value but reflects the credit value of everything entering into the trade relations of the members of society, thus permitting all credit values to be treated as relative to a common antecedent, and eliminates declared value by authority of government as a basis for comparison.

Government by this method becomes simplified as the economic system to a large extent governs society and takes from a government congress all discretionary power affecting people's civil liberties.

In people's contract relations it is futile to attempt to regulate the value of money as a thing existing by itself. The value of the monetary system can be successfully regulated only when considering it relative to its complement: the private ownership of land and its products. Since the two constitute the facilities that enable people to divide their labor—and then subdivide—then either becomes an integral part of the other, and both are necessary to complete the system of private ownership.

Because of the vagueness in the wording of the Constitution of the United States of America and the complete lack of knowledge of the principles involved in contract government existing at the time of its adoption and the beginning of its application as authority for government, the terms of the contract between the equity holders of sovereign ownership and private ownership were never established by the American Government Congress. Such lack of knowledge is apparent also in the people by their acquiescense in such acts of the Congress and, more especially, when later on such acts of the Congress were sustained by the courts.

It is not conceivable that an educated people would attempt to surrender their undefined equities in the sovereign ownership of every square foot of land and all products thereof in the nation to an agency and permit said agency to allocate to private ownership defined units of land in perpetuity, without first having the regulatory laws set forth in such way and manner as to protect for said owners of sovereign equities and their posterity the full benefits of their ownership.

The personnel of the signatories of the American contract is ever changing, and the generation living at any period of time cannot bind those living at any subsequent period of time from the benefits of their sovereign ownership. This is ethical and, as such, is therefore also logical.

Regardless of the fact that said equities of sovereign ownership have been disregarded in their entirety, the American people of today are in no way bound by the acts of their early Congresses and the decisions of the courts relative thereto. This is a political problem for society to decide for itself.

The Constitution of the United States of America is a living document and is the contract existing between the American people. The agency of government authorized by said contract is not a signatory to it. Therefore, it is within the power of the people of the American nation to make their own determination of the powers delegated to their agency. The interpretation that has been placed on the delegated powers of their agency of government has given them conclusive proof that said agency nor any branch thereof is a safe custodian of their civil rights.

In establishing the economics of sovereign ownership as the authority for self-government, societies throughout the world would be taking the most advanced step in human history. Its benefits to societies are unlimited. It cannot hurt any member of a society and would greatly eliminate poverty. As a policy for government, the magnitude of its importance dwarfs all other problems combined confronting societies and must not be left to the decisions of people's governmental agencies, as it is not within the province of said agencies to determine most political problems for the people.

It is quite conceivable that should this policy be adopted in, for example, the United States of America, that all other countries in the world would soon decide to phase out their present governments and adopt this system as their authority for government.

The theory that government is sovereign over people in their civil rights must be discarded, and people must be instituted in their proper sphere and accorded the opportunity of enjoying the liberties they have reserved unto themselves and where no one has economic power over them.

Regulatory laws that establish the economic system under a contract form of government may be captioned under such descriptive headings as: "Regulatory Laws," "Terms of Contract Between Sovereign and Private Owners of Land," "Regulation of the Value of Money," and "The Economic System or Corporate Bylaws," etc.

The use of the herein proposed economic system in the United States of America would abolish the present practice, in that country, of creating credit on the people's potential sources of wealth. In effect, it ties people's credits in money and their credits in commodities together. This is accomplished by the use of the regulatory laws in the regulation of the value of money and the commodities produced, which in effect become the debit base for the credit in money paid to labor. It makes it impossible to inflate the value of money at the expense of commodities or to inflate the value of commodities at the expense of money, because both of these are the credit for labor performed.

It establishes a ratio of exchange between those credits exemplified by units of the monetary system and the units of credit exemplified in commodities, and no amount of connivance or manipulation of money could interfere with the exchange of credit value—the reason being that once the regulatory laws are established by which the credit values of the products are determined, it would take from any and all political agencies the declaratory power to interfere with those credit values. Each of these regulatory laws is an integral part of the regulation of the value of the monetary system as a part of a concrete economic system and leaves it to the members of society to regulate the value in the units of money in their concrete credit values.

In permitting a government congress the use of discretionary power in declaring the regulatory laws affecting people's civil liberties, the people are permitting it the use of plenary power, which is the equivalent of sovereign power over them.

The term *discretionary power* means plenary power: to grant such power to a legislative body on the theory of representative government is, in reality, establishing a dictatorial government over people's civil liberties.

If people admit of discretionary powers delegated their agency of government over their civil liberties, then they must admit that they have no reserved liberties. Under the present interpretation of the delegated powers in the American Constitution, if there are those who contend that the people are the government and they need further proof that their agency of government considers itself sovereign, let them turn to the Bill of Rights, the first ten amendments to the Constitution which were adopted at the meeting of the first Congress of the United States of America in 1789.

The amendments follow closely bills of rights adopted by the different states that had adopted constitutions of their own following the close of the Revolutionary War. In particular, the amendments followed those of the Virginia bill of rights, in which there were nine clauses. The bills of rights adopted by the various states paralleled, in many respects, the Bill of Rights adopted by Great Britain in 1689, nearly one hundred years before a bill of rights was adopted by the central government of the United States. Under British form of government, the government is sovereign and is so recognized by the people.

In the United States of America, the natural limitation of the people's power, under a continuous contract, prohibits any possibility of conferring sovereignty on an agency of government. The American people need no Bill of Rights to tell them that they cannot enact certain types of legislation; therefore, the Bill of Rights in their Constitution is an unnecessary appendage.

It is obvious that the original American Congress had no intention of proceeding under the theory of contract government, and this policy has never changed.

In the interpretation made by the American Congress of its delegated power as representative of the people, it has usurped the power to establish policy in a manner of its own choosing; in so doing, it has disregarded entirely the equities of sovereign ownership of the sovereign people of the United States. This, the original interpretation, was and is the critical point in government. To disregard such equities is to establish autocratic government. To recognize such equities is to establish a true democratic or corporate form of government.

In order to have the benefits of true democracy, it is the privilege—and duty—of the people of the United States to inform their agency of government that the agency shall not have the plenary power to establish policy.

Should the people of the United States of America choose to abolish all the hazards of industry, commerce, production, distribution, and employment, which exist in the economy of private ownership, in favor of the economics of sovereign ownership that offers security, such is their right; it is of no concern to their agency of government as an incorporated body, nor any branch thereof.

In considering a contract form of government continuous in nature, one may turn wheresoever one may, always one is confronted with the limitations of the power of society to confer a plenary power over people's liberties, thereby binding future signatories to their contract out of their rights. The alternative to this form of government is to establish people under a system of regulatory or corporate bylaws.

The economic system is instituted by the use of two material factors, of which the private ownership of geographically defined units of land in perpetuity is one, and a circulating monetary system is the other. These two facilities are then caused to function by the use of four coordinated laws:

(1) commodity rate redemption law (price filing law)
(2) limitation of profit law
(3) commodity tax law
(4) pensioning system law.

These four laws constitute the fundamentals of a nation's corporate bylaws under the economic system. The purpose and effects of these laws in their relation to each other, and how they establish system to all of society, follow.

The purpose of the commodity rate redemption law is to have the commodity redemption rate of the product of all labor known in terms of its credit value, relative to the units of the monetary system, at the time the labor is performed in the production of same. This is necessary in order that labor may be credited at the time of performance and to insure that the credit in commodities corresponds with the credit in money.

Because of the manner in which the members of society have divided their labor in myriad divisions, and we are dealing only in commodities in this law, it is necessary to take one division of labor somewhere along the line between the production of the raw materials and the retailing of the finished product to the consumer, as a basis for the establishment of this law.

The logical choice of the various divisions engaged in this service is the manufacturing division. This is composed of millers, manufacturers, packers, canners, producers and processors of fossil fuels, and the producers of electrical energy. It is noted that this is the point of greatest concentration of raw material. The owner directors of this group compose a small fraction of a nation's total population. (Employees of this group do not set redemption rates.)

To understand the full meaning of this law, compare it to the power now exercised by the Congress of the United States of America to declare the redemption rate in gold of the country's currency. This power is taken from the Congress and is enforced upon the owner directors of the group, mentioned in the foregoing, to declare the redemption rate of every unit of commodity of given quality of their production in terms of money. In effect, this law establishes the commodity production of a nation as a unit credit value for labor thus performed in terms of credit value of money, which is held by all of society. It also places a blanket debit on all commodities entering into the channels of commerce. A blanket debit constitutes the claim of the members of society on goods in proportion to the credits in money a member presents for redemption and is, therefore, the motivating force that causes money to circulate.

In establishing this manufacturing group under a permit system, owner directors should be compelled to publicly file a schedule of the rate of redemption of each and every commodity of given quality of their production, said rate to remain in effect until such times as they may file a new schedule of their commodity redemption rate.

In establishing this group under a permit system, freedom of action should be given to change redemption rates of commodities at any given time by the owner directors notifying the government of rate change within fifteen days of effective date. After giving such notice and at the end of the time limit, with government approval and having double-checked for accuracy, their new schedule of prices shall become effective. Any deviation from this filed schedule of prices, for any reason, should be prohibited, and if persisted in by any owner directors, should result in revocation of permit.

The effect of this law is to establish those engaged in the wholesaling and retailing of goods on an essentially equal cost basis from which to compete in the merchandising of commodities.

Since the finished unit of commodities in the hands of the manufacturing group represents the credit value of their employee labor engaged in the reducing of raw materials to finished commodities, as well as all other labor engaged in the production of raw materials used, and transportation, then the filed redemption rate represents the accumulated credit value of those engaged in all of these industries. In this manner the relative values of all credits, including money, are reflected in units of the monetary system, thereby making all credit values relative to each other with no fixed standard as now exists in all countries.

The second regulatory law (limitation of profit law) is to establish a limit of profit which those in the manufacturing group shall be allowed under their filed schedule of prices. This action is necessary in order to prevent an excessive accumulation of credits with those of the manufacturing groups and cause a breakdown in the people's system of production and distribution of goods.

Profit, in the manufacturing groups, means that net income remaining after all costs in the manufacturing or production of goods, including tax, are paid for.

This profit should be on a graduated basis. To start this program, it is recommended that there shall be no limitation of profit on the sales of goods until a reasonable amount of profit has accumulated, after which 1 percent net profit tax shall be imposed on the sale of goods up to again a reasonable amount and graduated downward as the sales volume increases. (A government committee would establish guidelines under the limitation of profit law to allow for this.) Under this system, profits are to be calculated only on the sale of goods; capital investments are not to be considered as a basis for determining profit.

To those who might think that the recommendations herein set forth are entirely too radical a departure from the present methods, they should bear in mind the fact that the economic system is a system to insure to all members of society the benefits of their corporate equities and that industries and businesses of every nature exist by consent of the sovereign people.

The third regulatory law is a commodity tax law. In this law the present method of taxing potential wealth would be abolished together with all forms of capital tax, including license tax, and substitute, therefore, a commodity tax to be imposed upon those in the manufacturing group and added in their filed schedule of prices on a unit ad valorem basis similar to the gasoline and tobacco taxes of the present.

To inaugurate this program it probably would be better to maintain the income tax on all divisions of labor, and all of society is labor.

On those in the manufacturing groups, it should be abolished in its entirety because the limitation of profit law takes care of these. If, in the future, it should be deemed advisable to extend the profit limitation to all of society, then income tax should be abolished.

In this manner taxes are levied upon the wealth of a nation as it is produced, in volume sufficient to meet the needs of all of society under every condition of peace and war.

The use of this law would compel those engaged in the production and handling of goods to credit the labor performed by machine regardless of the source of energy used.

Since it is the credit value of labor that is being taxed, it matters not what form of energy is used—human, electrical, coal, water, atomic, etc.—the credit for labor thus performed in the production of goods must be given for distribution throughout society.

The fourth regulatory law is a credit distribution law, or more understandably called a pension law.

Under this law it is recommended that each person upon reaching the age of sixty will, should he choose to retire, be retired on a monthly pension. To the balance of society pensioning costs must be held relative to the crediting base of labor and must be based on the recipient's average monthly earnings of the twenty-year period prior to retirement (periods of illness not reducing the average). It is also recommended that a parent of retirement age, on pension, having the custody of children, be granted an additional amount for each child.

Since the economic system is the result of an agreement between the sovereign owners, none of society can be left without an income, except those in good health—mental and physical—below retirement age who refuse to contribute labor to the general welfare.

Under this system of establishing relative values, a check is imposed upon legislative bodies whose members feel disposed toward philanthropy by granting what they might think reasonable pensions to the aged for their own political advancement. Where this might occur, the producers of commodities may advance the redemption rate of commodities, thus holding all potential values relative to each other. It matters not what rate is established as a pensioning base.

Under contract government the right of the individual to a pension is his right to the benefit of his equity of corporate rights and bears no relationship whatever to a philanthropical act on the part of an agency of government or of a benevolent society.

Under modern methods of production, the full consuming capacity of the entire society of a nation is essential to a full-time employment of labor and of people's productive capacities.

In this manner people create demand and do not leave it to chance to create demand, as is the case under monarchical economy.

Demand is the consuming capacity of a people; their consuming capacity is a matter of their income or their ability to pay for goods to meet their desires.

This system displaces, in its entirety, the so-called natural law of supply and demand, because the factors that determine the value of goods are the factors that must be depended upon to establish values under the monarchical economy.

The economic system is not a leveler of income to the members of society, but it does have a tendency toward forcing a somewhat uniform income to the masses, with a distinction between the different classes of labor. Those of marked ability would naturally receive a higher rate of compensation for their labor than those less fortunate.

There would be no incentive for an employer to try to force the scale of wages downward, as the limitation of profit tax would prevent any gain to him by so doing.

Owing to flexibility in establishing the retirement age for pensioning, the competitive system in the labor field of today would change so that all surplus labor would be kept off the market, and the volume of labor for industrial and commercial purposes could also be regulated by putting excess labor on construction projects until they reach the pensioning age. As stated before, either way would cost the public nothing, based on the reasoning that pensions belong to that class of society that has been eliminated from work by the use of other energies, which is their corporate right.

Since the purpose of the economic system is to cause a reasonably equitable distribution of goods to all sovereign equity holders, then can it not be said that a liberal pension to the aged people costs the public nothing? Under a contract form of government, such as that under the Constitution of the United States of America, there is no method by which the rights of private ownership can be made to supersede the rights of sovereign ownership.

Because of the machine age and modern methods of transportation, farm products are lower in value today—relative to modern wage standards—than they would be if modern methods of transportation and machines were dispensed with and all such service were to revert to the methods of the nineteenth century.

A commodity tax imposed on commodities produced might possibly force some commodities as high, relatively, as would be the case were all produced by human labor, but people would still have the advantage of the lower prices of everything produced by the machines.

Regulatory laws are a system of limitation and the four regulatory laws enumerated earlier are first, to measure the unit volume of credit production and relative credit values of everything entering into trade relations—such as labor, services, property, and commodities; second, to prevent too great an accumulation of money by those engaged in the manufacturing group, who have by reason of the commodity rate redemption law been removed from artificial price-fixing competition owing to being on an essentially equal-cost basis; third, to credit labor performed by use of other than human energies harnessed and made to labor in the fields of production and distribution as an auxiliary to human labor; fourth, to distribute credit throughout society and thereby give people a complete economic system.

It is not the contention of this treatise that the laws drawn in this proposed manner will be sufficient to meet all of the needs of society living in the complex manner of the "machine age." It may be found, after a trial of these laws, that the limitation of profit will be found necessary to extend to any and possibly all of the various divisions of labor; then again, it may be possible to dispense with the limitation of profit law, in time, in its entirety by use of the unlimited monetary system. Keep in mind that money which is not directly representing units of labor performed to advance the economic welfare of society is political printing-press money and can only cause inflation and is therefore a crime against the people.

All of society is labor under contract government. Because of the ability to establish the age retirement and change said age at any time, society is given control over competition in the labor market. In case of an excess in the labor market, the pensioning age can be lowered, inducing some to accept pension in lieu of employment. If the labor market is short, the retirement age can be raised, thereby forcing those physically able to seek employment.

If labor is needed for government construction purposes and in building roads or other public improvements, said labor can, to a large extent, be made available through the adjustment of the retirement age limit. The cost to the public as a whole is the same, whether they are retired under a pensioning system or employed on public works.

The amount of money paid monthly, as a pension, although based upon average monthly earnings of the twenty-year period prior to retirement, should have a reasonable top limit. It matters not what average amount is set, because the credit represented in money is tied to the credit value represented in commodities; both are relative to the crediting rate of labor.

10

Effects

Accustomed as the people of the United States of America are to government under the interpretations made of the delegated powers in the Constitution of the United States, it is hardly conceivable that a change from this method could be made to one conforming with the interpretation of the delegated powers of their Congress given in this treatise without a long period of education of the people to this view, for it constitutes a complete reversal in the processes of government and of the rights of the members of society.

Since the states in forming the American Federation surrendered certain of their powers upon becoming signatories to the Constitution, those rights or powers were surrendered with the understanding that the interpretation made of the delegated powers of the Congress was correct; therefore, it appeared to the states that the rights or powers surrendered by them were fixed within reasonable bounds.

To change the interpretation thus made of the delegated powers of the Congress would require an entirely new interpretation of the power of the states to conform therewith. This becomes apparent in the right of any one of the federated states to tax.

Since the states surrendered any and all authority over money to the federated government of the states upon becoming signatories to the Constitution in order to have a unified monetary system common to all states, and since taxation is an integral part of the regulation of the value of money, then, in essence, the states surrendered all power to tax, subject to minor tax privileges allowed them by the Federal Government. And by the same token, all laws passed by the states conflicting with the economic system would of necessity become null and void. This, however, is not fatal to state government, as the residents of a state would lose nothing by conforming to the economic system.

In the matter of taxation, this could be adjusted in either of two ways: first, the federal government of the United States of America could exercise its power to levy and collect all tax and refund same to the states on a pro rata basis relative to the tax collected within each of the states; second, the federal government could first levy and collect all tax necessary to carry on the function of government as set forth in the economic system, then permit the states to add additional tax in an amount sufficient for their governmental functions.

In the matter of police power in the present interpretation of the delegated powers of government, either state or federal, it is difficult to state the limitation of power and the limitations of the rights of the citizens. In this twilight zone there seems to be no clear line of demarcation. In general, it can only be said that one's rights cease when the rights of society, as a whole, are adversely affected. This, however, is more or less a matter of degree and results in confusion to the members of society in not being able to determine for themselves the limitations of degree.

If a person feels that there has been an encroachment by others upon his rights or the rights of the public in matters of public safety, morals, etc., redress from same is sought in the courts. The courts, unfortunately, always have to sustain the police power of the state. Even though the case in question may be exceedingly doubtful, rather than the court jeopardizing its position with the public, it will recommend that the defendant seek relief from the legislative bodies. With this court assurance to support them, administrative police officers sometimes go to unreasonable lengths in the enforcement of police power.

This, for example, oftentimes happens to business firms engaged in processing foods. With such dictatorial powers, administrative officials cause, at times, unnecessary loss in foodstuffs, as well as the loss of reputation on the part of business firms by condemning plants, equipment, processes used, and even the products, thereby jeopardizing an entire business and causing the business firms great financial loss.

The purpose of the foregoing statement is not to defend unsanitary methods of preparing foods or the preparing of unfit foods to be sold to the public. It is rather to draw a comparison between the effects in the use of police power under present methods of procedure from the effects that would be produced under the interpretation as given herein, under the economic system.

Because of the limitation of profit on that class just mentioned in the handling of foods, the financing of improvements involved in plants of this nature could be paid for out of the tax assessed against them under the limitation of profit law, and if the tax were not enough to cover said expenses, the additional cost could come from the commodity tax and would not penalize the operators of food-processing plants. They would, therefore, be encouraged to conform to the most rigid sanitary laws.

For the purpose of enforcing sanitary regulations, all such business firms would come under a permit system, and the only penalty for nonconformance would be a revocation of permit.

License taxes, along with all other present methods of taxation, would be abolished.

In connection with this subject, the cost of the construction of all building and interior facilities would be financed by governments but to all intents and purposes would be privately owned and operated. Neither state nor federal governments would have any hand whatsoever in management or the pricing of commodities.

The reason for this is that the economic system is people's system for self-government in which they divide their labor into various divisions and carry on the processes of production of raw materials and the transportation of same to the various millers, manufacturers, packers, canners, processors, etc. The raw materials are reduced to the finished unit of commodity and are then transported for distribution through the channels of commerce. It is in these activities, including the various service organizations, that people perform their labor and establish the credit for said labor through the use of the economic system. To permit the agency of government to have a hand in the management of pricing of commodity would destroy the economic system and compel people to proceed by an economic method, dictatorial in nature, similiar in every respect to that which societies have been accustomed throughout the long history of government.

When commercial building facilities held by any individual are sold, a separation of the sale price of same from the land value of location should be made and the proceeds from the building facilities revert to the government. Since the government furnished the capital necessary for the construction, then, on selling same, the proceeds revert to the government. By the same reasoning, a prospective purchaser of any building facility, after purchasing the land through his own resources and upon making application to a state or federal government (whichever takes over the supervision of such), should be granted the money required to purchase the building facility thereon.

Living quarters to be owned by the individuals of society and the trading or bartering, or buying or selling of same is a matter that concerns only the people involved.

The foregoing proposed method of financing of building facilities for the manufacturing and processing of goods is offered only as tentative. As before stated there is, apparently, no theoretical limitation on the circulation and issuance of credit for labor, and the volume of money circulating as credits, and may therefore, cause people to resort to governmental financing of manufacturing facilities.

If through trial, it was found by society that there is no practical limitation in the issuance of and the circulation of money necessary as credit for labor, where same is circulated free of debt, as is contrary to the monarchical monetary system, then the limitation of profits could be greatly modified.

The Limitation of Profit Law is advocated as one of the four basic regulatory laws of people's corporate existence only for the purpose of inaugurating these by-laws for self-government. The Commodity Rate Redemption Law, the Commodity Tax Law, and the Pensioning System Law are the fundamentals upon which corporate government is founded, and the Limitation of Profit (tax) Law may eventually be eliminated.

This problem is one for future societies to determine for themselves because the effects of a monetary system of this nature are limited in their ramifications compared with the present monetary systems; still it is beyond our power to see its limitations.

To those of society who would lightly cast aside the theory of money circulating as credits for labor performed, without a debt (or debit), as being impractical and without merit, let them explain the justification for circulating money as units of value by reason of a debt (or debit) and by reason of a declaratory power of a government congress under a contract form of government where the liberty of sovereignty is not extended to posterity.

Any attempt to circulate money as units of value by reason of a debt, under constitutional government, is binding future sovereignty (people) out of the control of their property in favor of private ownership.

To try to justify the power of a government congress to

issue money with a declared value by reason of a debt, one must proceed from one of two premises: first, that the agency of government is sovereign and is, therefore, the absolute owner of every thing within the jurisdiction of the nation, and by reason of such, may declare any or every thing as a debt in order to give units of money value and bind posterity out of their liberty of sovereignty; second, that the agency of government, as a corporate body, separate and apart from the people, has the right and power to purchase and hold in corporate ownership any properties it deems necessary to declare as a debit in order to give units of money value, which is again denying to posterity their sovereign ownership in said properties.

This leaves people with no other choice than to circulate money debt free. Since they have no other choice in instituting a monetary system than one free of debt—other than a blanket debit in all of the products of labor—then the problem of circulating same becomes one of limitations. What and where must these limitations be placed? These are the problems for future societies to determine.

Many may consider the foregoing method of the transfer of property as being impractical in its attainment, but to deny such is to deny the sovereignty of peoples, because all capital, which is the product of land and labor, is owned in corporate ownership, as undefined and undivided equities of every resident of a nation. The fact that people have instituted a system of private ownership does not affect their corporate ownership, and, by reason of such, society has a right to establish the conditions of private ownership under which properties may be held, transferred, or utilized. Any attempt to divide such is, in effect, trying to bind the living generations and posterity from their equities of corporate ownership. All regulatory or bylaws must be made to conform to the relativity existing in the equities of corporate ownership.

Counties and municipalities may derive their income

from federated states on a pro rata basis of either per capita or sales volume of goods, or in any manner which they may choose, to allocate money for local government, which in any case would approximate the same.

Because of the effect of the limitation of profit law on corporations, the stock and bond market would be eliminated. There would be no necessity for the issuing of bonds to obtain capital, because people's agency of government would be in a position to supply ample capital, without interest charge, for the construction of facilities of any and every nature for the production of goods and for communications and transportation, etc.

Through the commodity tax, a government would always have a steady income to meet ordinary expenses of government and may carry a surplus in the treasury, but where an emergency may arise requiring a vast expenditure of money on the part of government, the same may very quickly be had, by an act of the government congress increasing the commodity tax at a rate sufficient to secure the estimated amount required. In such emergencies it would be best to give, temporarily, the government congress the police power to hold the rate of crediting of labor stationary, while advancing the redemption rate of commodities to the extent of the added tax revenue needed, thereby drawing the extra money from the public at large. Such power should be permitted only as an emergency power. This method of raising money would eliminate the issuance of bonds or treasury notes.

A government should not be permitted a voice in the management or operations of commercial facilities of any description, nor in the pricing of goods, labor, or services, for the economic system is a system reserved for the members of society for self-government, and it is not within the province of a corporate board, delegated with only regulatory powers, to interfere in the economic system. To do so, in any manner whatever, is an infringement upon the rights of the living generation as well as posterity.

Since industrial bonds of every nature are the product of the economy of private ownership and a declared value in units of money by government, said stocks and bonds of corporations would eventually become worthless.

Bonds issued by political bodies, such as federal, state, and municipal governments, are in a different classification from industrial bonds and are based upon the taxing power in the future of said political bodies.

As explained before, the power to tax under a contract form of government is an integral part in the regulation of the value of money, and this power has been delegated to the federal government of the United States of America. Each state or municipality in that nation is barred under the terms of the American Constitution, based upon this interpretation, from utilizing the power to tax; therefore, state and municipal bonds will have been issued without constitutional authority.

The potential value of the bonds issued by the American federal government would not be interfered with by use of a commodity rate redemption law forcing the potential value of property downward, because the bond value is based on present and future taxing power of the government; the limitation of profit law leaves no income for profit for the redemption of government bonds as would be the case with all industrial bonds.

While the potential value mentioned for bonds issued by the American federal government can be justified only because of the authority enumerated in the powers of the Congress—"to borrow money on the credit of the United States"—it cannot be justified by logic based upon the interpretation given herein of the delegated powers of the Congress, because the issuance of bonds of any nature is, in the final analysis, based upon the profit system made possible in the economics of private ownership.

It has always been assumed that people's agency of

government is sovereign over the individuals of society; therefore, said agency could be empowered to create a debt and compel posterity to liquidate said debt. In this concept we again meet with people's limitation of power under a contract and find it impossible to confer such power upon people's governmental agency. The powers conferred upon the American Congress to regulate the value of money in accordance with the interpretation of the Weights and Measures Clause, given in this treatise, are ample to permit the American people's government to meet any emergency without a debt.

To bring the outstanding indebtedness of a federal, state, or municipal government to a condition conforming with the economics of sovereign ownership of people, one of several ways may be used, either of which would effect the same end: namely, the elimination of wealth through the uncontrolled crediting and debiting of personal and real properties as exists in present monarchical type economies.

The use of any of these methods would be protested by the holders of bonds as being a confiscation of their wealth.

This argument cannot be considered valid when the economics of private ownership by the use of a limited monetary system is invalid.

The first method proposed is an outright repudiation of all bonds issued by political organizations.

The second method proposed is, by use of the commodity tax, to pay bonds off at their agreed valuation. To accomplish this, it may be necessary, as a temporary expedient, to limit the amount of capital in the form of money that anyone may hold. The purpose of this is to reduce the credit structure of wealth in a nation to a point well within the volume of money in circulation, since under this interpretation, the property wealth of the nation could not be used as a basis for credit. The monetary wealth of a nation is the amount of money issued by the government.

The effect on banking and insurance would have but

very little effect on society when removed from the economies of private ownership, but it would eliminate these institutions as they now exist relative to present economies.

Banks may be better operated by governments, for their function would be mainly that of a repository for privately owned funds which would be noninterest bearing or at a very low rate of interest.

It is proposed that all monetary capital become the property of the government upon the holder's demise, except and only when the holder is survived by minor children or wife or husband. Legacies should be limited to an amount of currency only sufficient to meet estate debts, and, if the legacy is large enough, an amount sufficient to reasonably support minor children and surviving husband or wife. Upon the demise of the direct descendants, any currency residue (balance) should become due the government. This limitation is proposed only on the monetary wealth of the deceased. Realty holdings are of no moment, and the holder thereof should be permitted to will them to those of his choice. Real estate is only the basis for the creation of wealth in the form of goods but not in the form of money, and it is of no importance to society who holds it.

The foregoing method of reducing the credit structure to within the monetary wealth of a nation as affecting government bonds is not any more severe on the holders thereof than would be the depreciated values back of the securities issued by industrial enterprises.

The reduction of credit wealth becomes a necessity by reason of the method given herein of regulating the value of money, as such were issued because of the profit system that exists at the present time; if the same is abolished, then the effects therefrom are dissipated.

Interest on money as a gain to the holder thereof would be nonexistent.

Commodity exchanges, dealing in futures, would automatically cease, as the exchange values of all commodities would be stabilized by use of the commodity rate redemption law and the limitation of profit law.

To those who hold that the economics of private ownership is necessary to encourage private initiative, let them explain by and under what authority the economics of private ownership can be established, under a system of government organized in such manner that the present and all future signatories to their contract, retain unto themselves their sovereign equities of ownership. Under such conditions, how can private ownership of property be made an absolute ownership?

To establish the economics of sovereign ownership by the people requires only regulatory power vested in its agency, as affecting their system of self-government.

Organization can exist only by an abridgement of the unlimited freedom of the individual.

The purpose of organization is to restrict unlimited freedom of action on the part of individuals; their remaining freedom becomes subject to the conditions of organization. It takes freedom from people's liberty of sovereignty to that existing by reason of the terms and conditions of their contract relations.

Where free enterprise results in economic power to the individual, such is an infringement upon the sovereign rights of others.

The stimulation of private initiative would be as great relative to the capital structure existing under the economics of sovereign ownership as it would be to the capital structure existing under the economics of private ownership, and it cannot, therefore, be deemed a valid reason for controversy on this subject.

In presenting the effects of substituting the economics of sovereign ownership for the economics of private ownership, one cannot escape from the basic rule of cause and effect: if the cause is removed, the effects cannot continue.

From this it would follow that by the elimination of the profit system, which now exists, with a corresponding restriction of the capital structure of wealth, capitalism as we have known it would disappear, and because of this, the former needs for commercial cooperatives would disappear; labor unions would exist not for economic reasons but for representation of workers to resolve social abuses caused, whether intentionally or unintentionally, by management of commercial enterprises.

Under the present economic methods, whether capitalistic or communistic, labor unions and cooperatives are a necessity in that they keep the wealth of nations more evenly distributed—more so than if the distribution of wealth were left to the agency of government subject to influences selfish in nature and financially detrimental to the people as a whole.

The responsibility for the interpretation that has been made of the Constitution of the United States of America and of its delegation of power and to the adherence to same, as the right of the American Congress to establish policy, must be that of the personnel that has occupied the office of the administrative, legislative, and judiciary branches throughout the history of government in the United States of America. All were under oath, individually and separately, "to the best of my ability to preserve, protect, and defend the Constitution of the United States." Hence, one is left no other alternative than to conclude lack of ability.

When considering the education of the society living at the time of the adoption of the American Constitution, one is inclined to feel more charitable toward the American people's apathy in permitting their leaders to place their own construction upon the delegation of power; nor is this an indictment against said leaders, because of their interpretation, as having ulterior motives for same. The history of the people of that period of time is ample proof of their integrity. Indeed, it may well be that the interpretation made and put into execution was better suited to the times and conditions of that period.

However, the American people of today, living in this

technological age of machine production and having the advantage of modern-day experience, are in a far better position to make an appraisal of their contract than was the generation living at the time of its adoption.

This modern machine age of production has brought to people new problems in distribution, unforeseen by those who interpreted the terms of the American Constitution.

These problems do not lend themselves to solution through laws based on tradition, and, as stated by Thomas Jefferson, "Laws and institutions must go hand in hand with the progress of the human mind."

Doubtless much opposition would be raised against change in the legal structure of the United States, as under such laws different classes of society have entrenched themselves in favorable positions to the detriment of the balance of society.

The effects produced by the present American legal structure have been, to quote Theodore Roosevelt, "to create malefactors of great wealth." They have been and are proving a great smoke screen for the real offenders. If any class can be deemed offenders, albeit unintentional, they are the members of the legal profession.

It is this class that makes and interprets the laws.

It is this class that is educated in the traditions and precedents of bygone generations of other nations, to which they steadfastly adhered when formulating and interpreting the American laws, disregarding entirely the people's contract relations.

It is this class that today is the most influential in determining the actions of society.

It is from this class that the personnel occupying the major portion of the legislative, administrative, and judiciary offices are chosen.

It is this class that has established the people's method of self-government and therefore their economy.

Since there is no real scientific information on the

sociology of laws, it is not surprising to find the members of the legal profession standing in the same relative position to the courts of today in asking of said courts an interpretation of the constitutional authority for laws governing the people—politically—as that of the high priests of Delphi in relation to the oracles, when asking of said oracles to ascertain for the high priests the will of the gods in matters affecting the well-being of the people of ancient Greece.

Just as the people of ancient Greece could not confer the power to ordain upon their mythical gods, neither can people of today confer upon their agency of government powers claimed by the courts.

The outstanding need of the peoples of all nations is a system of distribution to supplant the "law of the jungle" method in use at the present, with its inherent weakness to keep a method of distribution in balance with people's capacity to produce consumer goods.

The incapacity of those schooled in the traditions and precedents of other generations to institute a balanced system of production and distribution is apparent in the procedure of, for example, the American legislative bodies in the enactment of the class legislation of past decades. This legislation has been sustained by the courts, irrespective of the fact that the people of the United States are powerless, under their contract—which is their authority for government—to confer such power upon their legislative bodies.

Since the beginning of the machine age, people's system of distribution has lagged behind their methods of production, and apparently those schooled in the precedents and traditions of laws have nothing to offer that will keep their method of production and distribution in balance.

Since the production of the goods consumed by society by use of machinery was unknown to all people prior to the last few decades of the nineteenth century, it is futile to look to them for precedents and traditions that will furnish the key which will unlock the vast stores of potential production and will permit people to distribute same in their modern society.

To balance the distribution of consumer goods with the production of same, the units of people's money must be removed by the proposed regulatory laws from being classed as commodities in general.

Since units of money are the medium through which all consumer goods are distributed, to permit this specific class of commodity to accumulate in large volume in private hands by use of the profit system of the present, thereby permitting the holders thereof to collect interest for the use by others of same, seriously interferes with people's method of distribution of consumer goods, which in turn reacts on their ability to produce same.

To correct this inefficient method, the value of a monetary system must be regulated in such manner that the units thereof will reflect the labor credit value of everything entering into people's trade relations and circulated by use of a blanket debit on all consumer goods, thereby eliminating entirely credit by fiat of the governmental agency and also creating credit by use of specified debits in private contracts—such as notes, bonds, mortgages, and bank credits.

The term *consumer goods,* as used herein, includes all machinery used in the production and distribution of goods, and transportation and communication.

To enable one to make a comparison between present monetary systems, which circulate by reason of specified debts, and the monetary system given herein, which does not circulate by reason of a specified debt but rather because of a blanket debit on all consumer goods, the cardinal points of each system will follow.

First we will restate these important facts. There are but two kinds of monetary systems wherein the units thereof circulate freely between the members of society. In the first of these two systems, a plenary power to declare the value of the units therein must be vested in the agency of government. In the second system, only regulatory power is possible. The agency of government could not use a plenary power over the value of the units of money in this second system.

It is impossible for a society existing under a continuous contract form of government, as in the United States of America, to confer such power upon the government, except by abolishing private ownership and the government assuming the responsibility of the production of all consumer goods, in order to use such goods as a blanket debit for money. This would be approaching the conditions imposed in Marxist socialism.

The American Congress cannot, logically, be delegated the power to use the product of private ownership as a debiting base for the credits issued for labor performed under private ownership. When the employer, under private ownership, uses money as a credit for labor performed, the said employer must be compelled to state the redemption rate of that credit in the goods of his production, and it is the duty of the Congress to institute the necessary regulatory laws detailing the method of declaration of the redemption rate of goods in money in order that the credits for labor may be given the credit value of the blanket debit on all production.

Since money symbolizes credit and is used by all as their medium of exchange, said redemption rate of the credits is known in terms of all goods entering the channels of commerce at all times.

In the use of this monetary system, the credit values of money and the credit values of commodities remain parallel; neither one could fluctuate at the expense of the other. The reason for this is that they are both credits, and in their exchange relations they are equal in value. If the crediting rate of labor should increase, then the redemption rate of the product of labor may be increased proportionately. It is of no importance to society as a whole at what rate the crediting of labor is established, since the redemption rate of their credit would remain constant relative to the rate of crediting, giving people, theoretically, an unlimited monetary system in both the consumer goods redemption base and the rate of issuance.

The redemption base of consumer goods is like the mass of people forming society, in that it is constantly being consumed and as constantly being replenished and grows in its volume proportionate to the increase of population.

Although future society may find practical reasons for the limiting of the rate of issuance of money, in the light of present knowledge there appears to be no theoretical limit to its issuance.

It matters not the volume of money held by members of society in reserve, because it can be used at any time in the future at the then declared rate of redemption. If every member of society held currency in reserve, the redemption rate of commodities could not thereby be affected, because its rate of redemption cannot exceed the rate of consumption of commodities. The reason for this is that the crediting of labor by use of money as it is performed and the crediting of labor by use of units of commodity in its declared redemption rate remain equal, and unlike present monetary systems, the sale price of commodities cannot be fluctuated by reason of a necessary profit enforced, by reason of credit being created in private contracts and debited in specified property, subject to interest.

Where money circulates as credit by reason of a blanket debit, then said money is free from the obligations incurred in borrowing money under private contract and is, therefore, interest free.

A government congress should regulate the value of the monetary system as a facility for the crediting of labor, and since the crediting of labor exists in two forms of symbols—money and units of consumer goods, or commodities—then the producers of consumer goods must declare the crediting rate of labor in the units thereof. Said declared rate of crediting labor, which is the redemption rate of commodities in money, constitutes in the aggregate the blanket debiting base for money. In effect, the government congress regulates the value of the monetary system as a facility for crediting labor; the manufacturing group then declares the redemption rate of consumer goods in the units of money.

In the private ownership method of production and distribution of consumer goods and the division of labor in myriad divisions, the product of labor is the only thing people have that can be used as a debiting base to determine the credit value of their labor. Anything else used is an infringement upon the sovereign rights of posterity, because posterity cannot be bound to a debt for present people's convenience.

The importance of understanding the pricing of commodities, or the cost of same to consumers, is such that in order to make the distinction clear between present methods and that which would be effected by use of corporate bylaws, will merit the reiteration of the fact that the terms *price* and *cost* reflect 100 percent accumulated credit for labor, whereas in present methods of pricing, the same must include such items as rent, interest, and profit, including costs of production, transportation, manufacturing, packing, processing, etc., and including tax, with no discernible dividing line for each item, except as arbitrarily fixed items in bookkeeping.

Such is the effect of the use of a monetary system, limited in its volume and with an arbitrarily declared value by a government congress in the units thereof. Competition between individuals in conjunction with supply and demand has always been considered sufficient to keep prices on labor and the products of labor regulated within reasonable bounds. Labor in this context must be considered a commodity.

Since the postulate of value given herein, used in people's exchange relations, contains no other factor than labor, the cost or price of commodities represents 100 percent accumulated labor to the consumer. Each division of commerce adds the credit for their labor, as the commodities pass through the system of distribution.

It is therefore the purpose of corporate bylaws to keep the credit for labor as equitably divided as nearly as may be to all concerned in the production of raw materials—the manufacturing, processing, packing, etc., of same, and the tax for those not actively employed in production, because it is their right to a corporate equity of the products of all land and labor.

In presenting the effects that can be expected, if and when the interpretation given herein is adopted as the policy for governments, such as in the United States of America where government is based upon a constitution contract between the people, this treatise makes it clear that in pursuing the logic incidental to this interpretation its results would establish conditions foreign to people's former concept of government—but most beneficial.

Again, let it be clearly understood that there are only two kinds of contracts possible in formulating government, other than that form of absolute dictatorship government that results from seizure by force of arms and is established without a bill of rights or constitution contract.

The first interpretation is that sovereignty is in the government, and the second interpretation is that sovereignty is in the people.

It is obvious that this interpretation of the Constitution of the United States of America injects into the politics of the world an entirely new system of government, and there can be no illusions as to the difficulties involved in the educational processes required to instill confidence in the people to the extent that they would demand the adoption of this new interpretation.

Doubtless many people will feel shocked at the mere suggestion of the elimination of the profit system that has been used by societies throughout known history.

However, the use of the economic system is capable of compensation for all abuses existing in present economies. It will deprive individuals of the use of economic power over fellow members of society, and, by the same token, it will greatly eliminate poverty.

These two facts should be sufficient to encourage its adoption by societies throughout the world.

The use of the economy resulting from people's contractual relations in their sovereign ownership eliminates in its entirety the need to accumulate money to guard against poverty in old age.

People's monetary wealth, like their commodity production wealth, is consumed and created by society as they go. This is necessary in order to have a system of distribution of goods capable in its efficiency to utilize the products of the machines. People cannot have their monetary wealth lodge in private ownership and keep their commodity production wealth constant in distribution; each must accompany the other for efficiency in distribution.

The need for a system of distribution that will provide for all of society of any nation has always been the world's greatest need. Modern technology has become the means of making the subject of distribution more acute, and its solution is easily determined by use of the economy founded on the sovereign ownership by the people of any nation.

If society can be imbued with the idea that its membership is sovereign in their rights, powers, and ownership, and that they are so endowed by a power greater than man, and that by the very nature of the ever-changing personnel of their society they are powerless to surrender their sovereignty to an agency acting in the capacity of government, then possibly society can be induced to discard the laws enacted at the discretion of legislative bodies that do not recognize the sovereign ownership of the members of society; in so doing, it will enable itself to solve the problem of distribution.

The government of the United States of America, for example, as a corporate body, has no rights, powers, or privileges, which can be conferred upon the members of society. There is no method by which the agency of government could acquire such power. This statement will appear to many people as controversial, and they will argue that government does grant rights, powers, and privileges. The answer is that through the complaisance of the public their agency of government has usurped such power, and these acts are contrary to the oath of office—"to preserve, protect, and defend our contract"—which each officer of government must take. The people's contract does not call for usurpation of power over their civil liberty, for they have reserved all such power unto themselves.

To establish an economy founded on the equality of the members of society in regard to their mental and physical state of birth or development is manifestly dishonest.

To establish an economy founded on the equality of one's creation conforms in every respect to all moral philosophies.

In the field of industry, it would, because of the limitation of profit law, possibly cause a dissolution of the large corporations existing under the present economic method.

Income from investments may disappear to the point that such would no longer be a factor involving distribution of commodities.

It would not necessarily break up, or cause a suspension of, the vast manufacturing facilities in use at the present time, nor would it stop people from establishing other and greater facilities.

The economic system, once put into operation, is capable of caring for any number of society, and it matters not what source of energy is used in the production of goods—whether it is human labor or machine labor—the credit for the labor performed must be given and taken up and distributed in the manner proposed in the *economic system.*

There are no limitations in the economic system in its capabilities for curing the ills of society.

For instance, if it were possible for one man to produce all the commodities used throughout a nation by pushing a set of buttons, and another man could distribute all of the commodities so produced throughout the same nation by use of another set of buttons, society in any number could still live on any plane it chose to by the proper supervision and distribution of the units for labor performed. This, however, is a theoretical potentiality of the economic system.

Another spin-off benefit from use of the economic system is that, other than crimes of violence due to mental instability, the reasons for petty criminal behavior would be greatly reduced. By the same process of reasoning, all those who have been convicted of violation of laws not involving violence and are confined in penal institutions would eventually be discharged before previous parole date expectations, since the causes for possible repeat violations would no longer exist.

The use of discretionary power by legislative bodies in the enactment of laws affecting people's civil rights is the full use of sovereign power by said bodies. It is, therefore, the use of discretionary power that gives rise to a multiparty system of government.

Every society that is governed by a system of laws enacted at the discretion of its legislative body has an autocratic form of government, differing from each other only by degree.

There exist at the present time extreme totalitarian states based upon the ideology of Marxist socialism. The so-called democracies of the West—the United States of America and the British Commonwealth of Nations, etc.—are at the opposite sociological extreme. This latter group represents the most modified autocracies existing.

No national governments of the past or present recognize the sovereign ownership of all land by the people (Soviet Union not excepted because sovereignty is, in reality, vested in government).

Almost without exception, governments have disregarded and are disregarding corporate equities when instituting methods of private ownership of land. One cannot consistently disregard the immutability of effects from given causes nor the absence of same therefrom, when the causes are removed. It follows, therefore, that in regulating the value of people's money as a credit measurement under regulatory or corporate bylaws, the use of discretionary power by a government congress would be eliminated and the multiparty system would no longer exist as factors governing people's economy. The multiparty system of government was the outgrowth of the failure of the people's predecessors to realize or understand the nature of a contract containing millions of signatories involving a common sovereign ownership and the difficulties involved under such to institute a system of private ownership of geographically defined units of land in perpetuity and to regulate a monetary system in such manner that the members of society could use the units to express relative credit values of labor, services, properties, and commodities. These details were omitted in the original draft of the American Constitution contract and were left for the government congress to fill in by use of bylaws.

Since all of society of the present and of the future are equity holders in sovereignty, a government congress has no other alternative than to institute a system of private ownership to geographically defined units of land in perpetuity, subject to the equity rights in the products thereof of the holders of sovereignty of the present and of the future.

Once the details of the contract between the sovereign owners and the private owners of land are established by law, the government congress would have no discretionary power over people's civil rights.

Once the economic system is established through the use of the regulatory laws proposed herein, people will have succeeded in establishing themselves on as permanent a basis for government as is humanly possible and will therefore have much less use for legislative bodies.

In contract government, there is limited use for courts, because people's civil rights are adjusted by the economic system and will leave for the adjudication by the courts matters of criminal nature only.

It will greatly reduce the labor involved in administering civil law, for the economic system is almost self-administered. And because of the self-administering feature of the economic system, the need for members of the legal profession for every thing other than criminal law would be largely eliminated.

Other than acts of violence, which under all conditions are inexcusable, many crimes are the effect of causative laws. It would then follow that, by changing the causative laws, crime would be eliminated greatly.

Political activities of the future must be used to compel the personnel engaged in government to make a distinction between the two principles involved in instituting governments.

To construe a contract wherein all rights, powers, and ownership of sovereignty are retained in the body politic in the same light as a contract wherein the rights, powers, and ownership of sovereignty have been surrendered to a governmental body can no longer be tolerated by an informed society.

It is conceivable that posterity will credit fear of atomic fission weaponry and other destructive forces as the root cause of the elimination of selfishness from the world, whereas said selfishness is the product of the economics of private ownership administered by the use of discretionary laws of existing governmental bodies and can be eliminated only by future political education.

In the development of government of the future based upon the economic system, there will be sharply reduced adjudication by the courts of the civil affairs of the members of society.

Society can no longer afford to place its faith in the wisdom of the personnel of government and the rigid laws that are incapable of justice to all of society in a modern complex world.

To meet the complex conditions, it must turn to regulatory laws coordinated to such flexibility as will meet the needs of society, based upon the economics of equities of corporate ownership under contract government such as that which the Constitution of the United States of America authorizes.

As long as society permits the use of discretionary power to the personnel of government, it can expect to have dishonesty and political corruption existing therein. Financial gain to the personnel of government is just as enticing as it is to all others, even though it may be at the expense of the liberties of members of society.

There are no conditions in which society is justified in trying to divide its sovereign power over its civil rights with an agency, for throughout the history of mankind the wisdom of the personnel of government has not shown itself superior to that of intelligent members of society. To permit the personnel of government to proceed on the theory that said personnel, as an agency, is sovereign over society and that said agency can therefore bind posterity out of its liberty of sovereignty can no longer be tolerated as the fundamental upon which the principle of government is founded.

In reviewing the history of government in the United States of America, showing the trend of political action necessary to correct the faults of the people's methods of distribution of the products of human and machine labor, it becomes more clear that the governmental agencies are unable to grasp the complexities involved.

The American courts have sustained laws enacted at the discretion of the government congress that clearly violate the provision of the Constitution that guarantees the right of free speech. Yet because of the General Welfare Clause of the Constitution, the Congress and the courts pretend to perceive conditions wherein this prohibitive clause of the Constitution is not applicable.

The many laws passed by the Congress and sustained by the courts affecting the general welfare of the people, that are in violation of the principles of contract government, make it difficult to convince that the American people's courts are infallible.

As a protector of people's civil rights, the courts have proven themselves incapable and are therefore not qualified to hold the confidence of the public. In view of this record of the American people's courts, there can be little hope to adjudicate the differences that arise between nations. The economic problems that arise between the people of different nations are very much the same as the economic problems that arise between the people of the same nation.

If the adjudication of these problems, domestically, requires the economics of sovereign ownership of equities, then the same economic system will solve the differences between nations.

Since the question of sovereignty is involved in political problems internally and the problems arising between the people of different nations, and if people are sincere in their belief that "all men" are created equal economically and in justice, then logically "all men" must include all of all races and nationalities. Therefore, the sovereignty claimed by those of any nation over any given territory exists only by sufferance of those of all other nations, at any given time, for the people of any nation are not bound by the traditions or treaties of their predecessors.

At periods throughout recorded history the claimed sovereignty of the people of one nation over a given territory has been challenged by the people of another nation, who by force of arms have sometimes conquered and annexed the disputed territory, thereby increasing their productivity and enriching the conquering government. This procedure is more apparent when totalitarian states exist.

To prevent the claimed sovereignty over any given territory by the people of one nation from being challenged by the governments of other nations, it would appear that the approach to national security would be by international agreements to make the surplus foods of all nations available to any or all needy people. Said agreement should include surplus raw materials for manufacturing purposes. (This program must be implemented by rigid control of population growth.)

Since units of money, under the economic system of government, would be used to determine and distribute the benefits of corporate equities, such money would not be international in character nor does there exist at present any means by which said money can be made to balance with the declared value of the money of other nations. Such money circulates as units of value. The money of the United States of America, based upon the economic system, would circulate as units of credit for labor.

This would leave the American people with the problem of determining the utility value of goods in foreign exchange, and since there is no scientific approach to this subject at present logically established, exchange of goods between the people of different nations had best be based upon the needs of any people, without regard, for the present, to standards existing for balancing the utility values of the goods in foreign currencies.

Doubtless this would leave the United States government in the position of having to donate much of its surplus foodstuffs and raw materials to the people of less fortunate nations, which would be the price that it would pay for national security. It would be much like a rental paid to all of the people of the world in order to have them respect the rentor's sovereignty—a reasonable price to pay for national security.

The bartering of surplus goods between the peoples of different nations should be handled through their governmental agencies, because no man has the right to take the people's natural resources, raw materials, or foodstuffs, which are under corporate ownership, and sell them abroad for personal gain.

This method of barter would not draw the metallic gold or silver base of monetary systems of one nation to that of another and would leave monetary systems intact.

Since all of the people's natural resources are corporately owned, then by what means of reasoning can there be justified an act of a government congress authorizing class legislation of such nature as utility monopolies and farm cooperatives and authorizing same to establish themselves in a dictatorial position relative to the balance of society? In a logical economy, people would not permit their government congress to establish any fixed point in money or labor. Neither can there be permitted an authorization for minority groups to cause any fixed valuation of their labors.

If the existence of atomic fission, germ, and nerve gas weaponry with known potentialities for destructive purposes will suffice to teach the people of all countries that there is no method by which they can surrender their sovereignty safely to an agency established for the purpose of government, then these weapons will have served their most useful purpose.

11

Natural Resources

Instituting the economic system of corporate government, thereby eliminating the profit system resulting from a limited monetary system, would, to a large extent, conserve natural resources and prevent the waste of such.

The holders of timber, mineral, coal, and oil lands could not receive a profit on the products therefrom by exporting them in foreign trade, because these products are corporately owned and when they are sold in foreign trade the sale can be consummated only through an agency of the corporate government.

Because of the stabilizing effect of the commodity rate redemption law, the sale value of land, regardless of its classification, could not be fluctuated. This is based upon the theory that land is worth what it will produce and the value of its production is what it will bring on the market for same. It follows, then, that if the value of raw material is controlled through the commodity rate redemption law, the sale value of property would become stabilized relative to the sale value of its production.

The practice of exploiting natural resources for export in foreign trade is not a basic necessity in the economic system, since in said system people are dealing in credit of their own production.

People living under the economic system are not involved in the units of value in circulation in other nations. To bring such into their country would fall outside of their economic system and would not have a controlled redemption rate in the articles within their nation's geographical boundary. (Various nations adopting the economic system could coordinate their units-of-labor valuations relative to commodities.)

No one would have a right to sell resources of the nation to a people of another nation without the proceeds, less the costs involved from said sale, becoming the common property of the corporate owners.

The importers of foreign goods into the nation, under the economic system, would be classed in the same bracket as those in the manufacturing group and be compelled to list their redemption rate of goods in money, and their products would be taxed the same as domestically produced goods. The purpose of this is to bring the units of commodities of foreign production in line with the potential credit value of domestically produced goods and establish the credit rate of said goods relative to the currency of the economic system.

Insofar as the economic system is concerned, it is of no importance whether goods are produced by the lowest priced physical labor in countries not based upon said system or whether goods, of domestic or foreign manufacture, are produced in part by the harnessed energies of nature.

Society, in any volume of members, can live comfortably by the proper supervision of credit given for labor performed, in both the credit symbolized by money and the credit symbolized by commodities, and by the proper distribution of same throughout the society. Since the credit value in money for labor performed equals the credit value in the products of labor in the economic system, said system has no limitations in its ability to care for society.

It is of little moment who owns the land in private ownership, since the credit value of money equals the credit value of commodities in the economic system, and none can receive a greater and excessive profit from same at the expense of the balance of society—other than that small profit provided for in the system—because the economic system is not and should not be an exact equalizer of income to all.

Under present procedure, any profit that may accrue to one must necessarily be as a debt to others, therefore, there is the necessity for a profit system to meet said debts.

By use of the corporate economic system, the total of all wealth of all of the people can be no more than the value of the land, with its improvements, of the nation, stabilized through the commodity rate redemption law, plus the total money in circulation and goods produced.

The only debt existing would be the relationship between all goods produced and money. Even here it is not a debt as people understand a pledged debt by private, corporate, or government contracts. Though the goods produced and money are both credits for labor performed, neither of these credits is pledged as a debit to the other, but either may be resolved into its opposite as the option of the holder.

In the case of the United States of America, it would eliminate entirely the credits now existing based upon inflated valuation of property, both personal and real, and the debt existing because of government's —federal, state, county, or municipal—debiting of future taxing power.

It amounts to a system wherein the residents of a nation pay as they go. Any emergency needs that may arise in meeting the costs of government, as in the case of war, could be fully met and paid for on a cash basis by raising the commodity tax to the amount necessary to meet such needs.

This could not disturb the economic system, because the redemption rate in goods would immediately be broadened to cover the circulation of money by broadening the field of taxation to cover the emergency-produced goods.

In following the reasoning of this theory of government, one should always bear in mind the highly important fact that it is the industrial and, in general, production groups of the nation, charged with declaring the redemption rate of goods in terms of money, that establish the basis for creating credit for labor, and not a government congress.

Since taxation is an integral part of the regulation of the value of money, the power to tax is a function permissible only to the government. When the agency of government, in order to meet an emergency of any nature, deems it necessary to increase the rate of taxation to finance said emergency, then the industrial groups of the nation may at their option change the redemption rate of commodities to money to correspond with the new rate of taxation and collect same on a pro rata consumption basis from all of society. As compensation to society, all of its members are guaranteed an income in sufficient amount to meet their costs of living, taxes included.

It should be remembered that the rate of commodity redemption is the credit value claimed by the producers of commodities for their labor and are therefore redeemable in the credit value of money.

Any change that may occur at any time in the rate of redemption of commodities cannot result in added profit, because of the limitation of profit law.

To those who believe that this system would destroy private initiative, it must be remembered that people hereby are dealing in a contract form of government based on equality of sovereign human rights and that there need not necessarily be a limit of one's reward for private initiative. People may be stimulated, if stimulation by profit is necessary, through the moderate profit system, as proposed and instituted through the economic system.

In considering the stimulation of private initiative as an attribute of the present profit system, we should also consider that there are disadvantages that accrue from this illogical profit system such as deception, dishonesty, poverty, and even crime, which more than nullify the advantages. People can only question, therefrom, if the unlimited profit, from a limited monetary system, is necessary.

Contract government cannot be construed as embodying a profit system as people now have it.

The adoption of the economic system would quickly eliminate the capitalist class because of the elimination of all property-debiting bases for credit, and credit for labor would become the only form of credit existing.

The inflated value of property, either personal or real, which is the debiting base for much of present accumulated wealth, would collapse and cause said properties to decline in value—relative to their productivity; and other credit, created and based on the future taxing power of federal, state, and municipal governments, would be eliminated.

Because of the foregoing reasoning, there would be no further reason for labor organizations to struggle for a more equitable distribution of wealth, and their reason for continued existence would be mainly of a social nature to mediate disputes between commercial management and labor.

Cooperatives, either farm cooperatives or otherwise, when made by law a part of the basic economy, become class legislation and dictatorial to the balance of society, and these would become unnecessary. The reason for their existence in European nations is that Western Europe is made up of a multiple of small nations—none of which are self-sustaining in regard to present living requirements. The living standard of the people of these small nations is dependent upon their foreign trade. Cooperatives as a part of their economy are based upon the power created in these organizations to bargain, advantageously to themselves, when dealing in the commodity products of labor with the people of other nations.

Because of the limited resources of these nations, the variety of commodities produced by each nation is limited. Of the commodities produced—in far greater volume than the people have ability to consume—the balance is sold in foreign markets.

In pooling these commodities into a small number of

selling agencies, a decidedly better advantage in dealing with the people of other nations is obtained. It cannot be denied that this procedure results in a benefit to the members of the cooperatives and indirectly to their nations.

When comparing the political theory of cooperatives and labor unions, we should remember that both of these sociological divisions are organized for the benefit of their respective membership and that the purpose is to gain a greater return on the products of their labor.

In transplanting these two sociological divisions of essentially European origin and making each a part of the basic economy of the United States of America, little consideration was given to the fact that the people of the United States are residing in an almost self-sustaining nation, in which the people produce and consume, under normal conditions, far the major portion of their production.

The American people have, comparatively speaking, little of their production to deal with in foreign trade; therefore, they are in no position to make the people of foreign nations pay high income to labor unions and cooperatives. High income to these organizations, when dealing in domestic trade, must come out of the pockets of the balance of the American people, who are not favored by such protective laws.

Because of the fact that a government congress would have a free hand to regulate the retirement age, thereby permitting excess labor, both men and women, to accept a pension should they so desire, the total labor volume can at any time be adjusted to the demand for labor.

With no excess labor on the market and the fact that employers could not reap profit by holding the wage of labor down, labor, as a group, would have no reason to be doubtful of receiving a fair share of the wealth of the nation.

Thus the advantage to labor is far greater under the economic system than it can ever hope to be solely under the regulation of labor union organization in present economies, because each member is entitled to, and would get without question, the benefits of his equity of sovereign ownership.

Under contract form of government, no division of industry or labor can be permitted in any respect to organize and pool their resources under private ownership to gain an advantage and secure for themselves an unfair benefit from their equity of sovereign ownership relative to the balance of society.

12

Control of Production and Distribution

The economic system would give people effective control of the production and distribution of goods, both consumer and capital, so that millers, manufacturers, packers, canners, processors, and producers of coal, oil, and electrical energy, etc., would be limited in their purchases of raw materials to the actual sales of their products. This would be done by imposing a commodity tax upon this group, based on the unit of commodity of given quality at their filed redemption rate with a limitation of profit thereon. Said tax would be subject to collection at the time of the sale of the commodity or at stipulated intervals or not longer than each calendar month.

This would have a tendency to leave surplus raw material at the point of production. Compensation to the producers of unsold raw material is made by the elimination of present taxing methods, such as land, livestock, farm implement, and school taxes. The pooling of agricultural products for sale may be made through cooperative associations. In this respect it would probably be better to limit the activities of cooperatives to that of collection agencies, and they would remit to their membership on a pro rata basis the proceeds from the volume shipped, relative to the entire market sale for same in any given community. The idea here is to provide a method by which all producers of agricultural products may receive the benefit of the market of their production proportionate to the sales as a whole in any given community of any given commodity.

If cooperative associations act in the capacity of millers, manufacturers, packers, canners, or processors, or any other activity controlled by the commodity rate redemption law, then the same would have to conform to the provisions of this law on the same basis as all others and be limited in the profit on the sale of goods sold.

In limiting the profits to cooperatives that enter into the field in competition with those in the manufacturing group who are, in most cases, the customers of the cooperatives for raw materials, a dividing line in the monies returned to its membership and the total income to the cooperative should be made on the basis of the price of the raw material sold to the customer of the cooperative.

The term *customer of the cooperative* in the foregoing paragraph means the numerous individually operated industries that purchase their supplies of materials for processing, etc., from the cooperatives.

If the cooperatives claim the right to mill, manufacture, pack, can, or process the raw materials of their membership's production, then said cooperatives must enter into the labor market, and by hiring labor, they will reduce their raw product to finished units of commodities. The profit on this part of their operation is taken on the labor they hire from the labor market, the same as with any other organization that purchases raw materials from the cooperatives and reduces same to finished units of commodity; they should be taxed on the same basis.

In many respects, farmers would be exempt from the commodity tax law because they consume much of their own production—not only the production for table use but also in the purchase of grain and other foods for feeding and seeding purposes; all of these should be exempted from the commodity tax.

Under this system there is no incentive for manufacturers to force down either the buying price of raw materials or the wages paid to labor, because these costs are calculated in the manufacturing group's filed redemption rates.

The commodities in the hands of those industries contained in this manufacturing group are the evidence of their credit for labor in exactly the same sense that money is the evidence held by all of society and is its evidence of credit for labor.

The value of these credits is determined by the ratio of exchange of these two different evidences of credit.

In case of collusion between those in the manufacturing group and the producers of raw materials to pay an unreasonably high price for raw materials and to divide overpayments between them to gain more profit, it would be a simple matter to extend the limitation of profit law to cover the producers of raw materials, or any other division of labor, that might try, through connivance, to attain profits beyond their just share.

Government by use of corporate bylaws is very easy to understand, once a person grasps the problems involved in each of the four basic principles given in the economic system, and, as mentioned before, other supporting laws will be found necessary.

In the sale of flour for baking purposes, flour millers should be held responsible for the tax on all packaged products sold retail to consumers. Where flour is sold for remanufacturing purposes—such as to bakeries and others—then said manufacturers must come under the commodity rate redemption law and be held for the commodity tax, because they must enter into the labor market, both manual and mechanical, and add labor to flour in its finished product.

Sugar offers another example where the tax must be transferred from the sugar manufacturer to the remanufacturer, such as candy and ice cream manufacturers and the fruit-canning industries. Here again these remanufacturers enter into the labor market and add labor to sugar, much of which is machine labor and must be held for the commodity tax.

The metal, cloth, and all industries where refined raw materials are used for remanufacturing would have to be made subject to the same conditions as the foregoing stated industries.

The theory is to include machine-produced commodities within the labor crediting base. This can be accomplished by use of the commodity tax law. Fossil fuel products and electricity come within the foregoing category.

Society of the future must be on the alert to broaden the field of taxation by including as much machine labor as is possible to assess, through the commodity tax law. In theory, a commodity tax is basically a tax on labor and is collected, both directly and indirectly, through the use of commodities. Bear in mind the fact that under a corporate form of government all of society is labor and that every member of society is a consumer.

The limitation of profit does not permit the collection of rental or interest on money. Those having private ownership of capital, in the form of either money or buildings and equipment, are not entitled to a greater right than those without capital.

Keep clearly in mind that, in contract government, members of society are dealing in their corporate ownership rights; therefore, all legislation must be made relative to this fact rather than to their private ownership rights.

The economics of private ownership under an autocratic form of government, whether state ownership *in the name of the people* (Marxist socialist) or capitalist, will not suffice to meet the needs of society and the conditions existing in this technological age.

To meet such, people must resort to the economics of their sovereign rights under a contract form of government.

The Constitution of the United States of America, when rightfully interpreted, gives ample authority to permit the people of that nation to meet their conditions and needs in this ever-changing world at all times.

The economic system, based upon the rights of equal equities of corporate ownership, establishes a system of self-government whereby all may receive the benefits of their equities, also a reward for private initiative, and establishes an effective control over the production of raw materials and the distribution of the commodities produced therefrom. It should not be confused with any theory of a planned economy emanating from socialist philosophies: such theories are presented as an idea of some individual or group who would attempt to correct present socioeconomic maladjustments by vesting more power in government.

People do not need the political ideologies of their predecessors or the political ideologies of an origin of a dictatorial nature, because none of those take into consideration adequately the conditions caused by the modern machine age. Neither do they take into consideration the fact of the lack of logic, under any theory of government, that causes members of society to surrender their sovereignty to an agency and, by so doing, to bind posterity from their equities of sovereign ownership, thereby permitting their agency to establish a system of private ownership of land without an accounting to the people.

The answer to the problem is not in depending on the wisdom of the personnel of an agency to adjust matters political but rather is in the withdrawal of power from the government agency by establishing a system controlling the principle of equality of people's sovereignty.

It is not only in the field of economics that government agencies, throughout the world, have demonstrated inability to construe a contract of the magnitude of the Constitution of the United States of America. They have demonstrated and are demonstrating to all people inability to deal with other nations logically in foreign affairs.

People are now fully aware of the power involved in

atomic fission, and what more may be developed in the future for the purpose of warfare destruction is at present unpredictable.

The leading governments of the world may succeed in arriving at decisions on matters that to them will appear ample to protect the rights of the people of all nations at the present time. The history of government is proof of people's insecurity when depending upon peace treaties. The weakness in present attempts to establish peace treaties and to accompany said treaties with an international banking system in accordance with the agreements arrived at, for example, in the Bretton Woods and Dumbarton Oaks Conferences, is that the monarchical monetary system is to be used therein. This system carries with it the economics of private ownership, in which the value in the units of money is dictated by an autocratic power and bears little relationship to labor and the products of labor. Thus the equities of sovereign ownership by the people of all nations are ignored.

As long as the monetary systems of the present are used by the various nations of the world, there can be no hope for permanent peace.

The reason for this is that in the present concept of value, when carrying on the trade relations between the people of the many nations, it can extract the very economic lifeblood of smaller nations' circulating monetary systems. This is done by demanding that the settlements in international trade relations be made in gold, or any other thing or things of value used as a debiting base to give value to their money.

The society of any nation cannot afford to delegate their sovereignty to an agency of government, because the world has thus far failed to produce a man or a body of men capable in wisdom, vision, and integrity to guide the destiny of a nation in a truly logical manner.

The society of any nation cannot afford to divide its sovereign power with an agency; to do so is to lose it all.

The societies of all nations cannot afford to vest in their respective agencies of government the privilege to declare war, for such power is not safe in the hands of an agency of government and must be reserved by the societies of every nation unto themselves. In this manner the challenge to physicists and engineers of the different nations to outdo each other in creating implements of warfare can be better directed to the economic welfare of all mankind.

In the present state of world affairs, which is the result of the inability to analyze the organization for government based upon absolute equality of rights of the members of their respective societies, people cannot stop in the race for armed supremacy to defend themselves in case of possible attack. Unfortunately, people must, at the present time, extend to agencies of government police power to raise and equip military establishments with implements of war until such time as the leading nations of the world can be made to realize that sound government can exist only in the corporate state; politically speaking, the domino theory here would apply, and the smaller countries would follow suit.

The adoption of the method of regulating the value of money as a labor credit measurement, as recommended herein, would bring many benefits to the members of society. It would be impossible to enumerate them, because it would enter into every phase of human activity. Following are a few of the more outstanding benefits.

In the matter of public health, it would abolish malnutrition in those individuals who are unable to find jobs with salaries adequate in value relation to commodities.

Hospitalization for the sick and incapacitated could and should be at the expense of the state.

As understood at the present time, expense as applied to money is money paid out from income limited by chance. Chance, as used herein, is controlled by the volume of money in circulation, which in turn is governed by the wage scale of labor and the commodity price level, together with the rate of creating debt credit and the inequalities existing between the members of society in their physical or mental development, sickness and accidents, which leaves them at a decided disadvantage.

Whereas in an *unlimited monetary system,* circulating because of a blanket debit in the products of all labor entering into the channels of commerce, expense has a different significance; it would mean in the case of government expenditures the enforcement of a greater volume of credit on labor performed because of the power to tax.

In the *limited monetary system,* used throughout the world at the present, expense comes from savings of the members of society. In the unlimited monetary system the savings of the members are not involved; people create and consume both their primary and their secondary wealth as they go. People's primary wealth is the commodity production of the nation; their secondary wealth is credit for labor performed.

The facilities and services required in hospitalization are a matter of public health and should be made free to all members of society. The right of the individual to choose a doctor because of personal preference is a right that does not concern the state. This is a minor example of where the state has the power to regulate civil rights but not the power to prohibit the use of same.

Schools of higher learning should be made free for all on the basis of competitive entrance examinations. Even costs of room and board for all students should be borne by the state.

Since the pensioning law is an integral part of the regulation of the value of money, poverty would also be abolished for the elderly. The power delegated to a government congress to regulate the pensioning age and pension monetary values makes it obligatory for the congress to see that all elderly members of society have the benefits of their corporate ownership.

The amount of wealth that the individual may accumulate in the modified profit system, incidental to enterprise of any nature, is unforeseeable. This is dependent upon profits permitted by future society. In any event, the holders of accumulated wealth could not have economic power over anyone.

The modified profit system would not necessarily interfere with the present state of the private ownership of land. It would abolish speculative values in land, because when the products of land are used as credits for labor, land values automatically become stabilized.

Because of the stabilizing effects of the commodity rate redemption law and of the low profit, it would reduce the rental values of land in the sense that the speculative value of the product of land would not exist; therefore, the speculative value of land would be nonexistent. Also, because of the elimination of the property tax, it may be found advisable to put the renters of property under the limitation of profit law.

The economic system need not cause any transition change in present monies; the same could be utilized as at present. It is only the corporate bylaws that would be established that would cause a change in the relationship of money to commodities.

The agency of government has not the right to institute itself in business of any nature to compete with business in private enterprise, not even for special reasons—with the exception of threat of war—because such would be an infringement upon the civil rights of the ever-changing personnel of society.

It is within the province of the people to permit their agency of government to enter into construction enterprises of such nature as road-building, dams, irrigation projects, and others of similar nature too massive to be handled entirely by private enterprise; they should not, after completion, be operated by government in competition with private enterprise.

To institute the foregoing described system of government, it is quite probable that much of society would see only modest change in their daily lives.

There is no need for force of arms to overthrow government, because any philosophy of government that is not sound enough to win its way by force of logic and justice to all humanity is not worth the price of revolution and bloodshed.

While the theory of corporate government is revolutionary in the extreme compared to that of accepted principles of government, yet it is capable of being instituted because of its soundness and its capacity to insure justice to all mankind.

Any philosophy of government in which the economy and the civil liberties of members of society are involved and which does not take into consideration the relativity of human rights in the ever-changing personnel of same and which denies the sovereignty of society over government cannot be deemed a sound basis for political structure organization.

As long as people permit themselves to be governed in matters affecting their economy and their civil rights by laws enacted at the discretion of legislative bodies and accept the opinions of law courts as to the right of said legislative bodies to enact such laws, society will be held static relative to advancement in logical governmental procedure because they are chained to the tyranny of precedent and tradition of monarchical government. Evolution is not dependent upon being chained to precedent and tradition, otherwise the human race would today be in the same state of development, both physically and politically, as were those of the Pleistocene epoch.

There is not, nor can there be, a more effective barricade to progress in matters political than being chained by laws that were enacted by and are governing people by reason of precedent and tradition. It is the postulate of people's inalienable sovereignty and the postulate that values exist only in their potentialities and that their relationship can only be expressed at any instant of time that opens the way to logical progress in matters political, and effectively destroys impractical government based on laws in accordance with precedent and tradition.

Doubtless, this accusation of existing tyranny will cause many people in the United States of America, when comparing it with the oft-quoted oath of Thomas Jefferson—"I have sworn on the altar of God, eternal hostility against every form of tyranny over the mind of man"—to wonder if Jefferson were secretly condoning tyranny while openly condemning it. Or perhaps, which seems more logical, Thomas Jefferson spoke in all sincerity, while not fully understanding origins of political tyranny.

The history of Jefferson's activities, in connection with the American government, will satisfactorily clarify this point. He was an ardent supporter of the Republican form of government. To him is credited the use of the decimal monetary system in the American nation. He was convinced that government had the inherent power to state the value in the units of the monetary system in either a silver or a gold basis. He was a champion of states' rights and the states' sovereignty as opposed to the federal central government in all matters not specifically set forth in the American Constitution.

It is only in regulatory or corporate bylaws based on relative factors of potential values used in exchange of ratios that true values are expressed and, as first postulated in this treatise, that the tyranny of precedent and tradition over the mind of man becomes apparent. It is, therefore, to the credit of Thomas Jefferson that he was only unwittingly condoning that which he so strongly condemned.

During the first one-and-a-quarter-century history of the American government, the term *democracy* was seldom used as descriptive of its form of government; rather, the term *republic* was the accepted description and was used almost exclusively throughout the states. It was, perhaps, mainly through the efforts of Thomas Woodrow Wilson, twenty-eighth president of the United States of America, that the noun *democracy* was popularized and substituted for the noun *republic*.

In analyzing the present form of government in the United States of America on the basis of the people's inalienable sovereignty, we find that Jefferson's choice of nouns was correct (*republic*).

In a republican form of government, government exercises the power to declare the value of the units of money and does not recognize the equity rights in the sovereign ownership of the land by the citizens. It is the most modified form of autocratic government. Monies are circulated as value measurements.

A true democracy is a corporate form of government wherein the citizens' ownership of corporate equities of land is recognized and monies are circulated as credit for labor measurements and without a declared value by authority of a government congress, thus making a complete distinction between the nouns *democracy* and *autocracy*.

13

Summary

The government of the United States of America, as a constitutional form of government, has been generally used in this treatise as an example for comparative purposes because its government, based upon a detailed constitution of specific sociological rights, is more easily explained as a contract among the people of a nation.

From the beginning, the intent of this treatise has been to adhere strictly to truths as such have been found through research of the basic principles encountered by peoples in establishing governments for themselves.

To arrive at the conclusions given herein is a radical departure in every respect from the accepted sociological concept dogmas of former generations, appertaining to political science and economics.

The people of the United States of America can accept the high ideals set forth in the founding fathers' Declaration of Independence as being basically sound, but they must question long-accepted interpretations of their government constitution in some important areas.

For example, sociologists cannot point to a single principle in justification of the long-accepted interpretation that has been made of the delegation of powers contained in the American Constitution. Nor can they, by the use of principles, disprove the fundamental truths set forth in this treatise used as the basis for a more logical interpretation of the delegated powers of the government congress.

The following fundamentals are submitted as a basis for

political change, and they will be readily apparent to all as being a complete reversal in generally accepted processes of government.

First of these truths (from the American Declaration of Independence): "that all men are created equal, that they are endowed by their Creator with certain inalienable rights, that among these are life, liberty and the pursuit of happiness." It will be remembered, as stated in the beginning of this treatise, that there is only one qualification possible to this attainment—all men are created equal in their rights and ownership of sovereignty. This fact alone precludes any possibility of the delegation of people's sovereignty, or any portion thereof, to an agency for the purpose of government. The foregoing statement is based in logic upon the ever-changing personnel of the signatories to their contract, in which none can sign away the sovereignty of others, thereby leaving all mankind with inalienable sovereignty.

It will be observed in the foregoing statement that no mention is made of the physical or mental state of one's birth or development.

Since the American people's contract of government is based upon the recognized principle of equality of man's creation, i.e., the equality of man's sovereignty, then in order to be consistent with this principle and because of the ever-changing personnel of its members, society has obligated itself to extend this franchise to all posterity.

To do so, certain rights, powers, and ownership are permanently entailed to itself and cannot be delegated to an agency of government. To attempt to do so is an attempt to bind posterity out of their sovereignty and is an attempt to destroy their franchise of liberty.

To confer a power on an agency of government, society must first surrender the corresponding liberty.

Second of these truths: the Constitution is a contract existing between the sovereign people of the United States, is continuous in nature, and makes every child, at birth, in effect, a signatory to it, and in which provision is made for an agency endowed with such powers as will enable it to carry out and enforce the terms of the contract. Said agency is divided into three branches, with the necessary duties and powers prescribed to each.

In matters appertaining to criminal law and foreign affairs, the government congress is endowed with plenary power.

In matters appertaining to civil law, the laws affecting people's civil liberties, the government congress is endowed with regulatory power only.

The fact that this is a continuous contract that recognizes the sovereignty of all people to come precludes any possibility of a society living at any given time from delegating sovereign power to its agency of government over the people's civil liberties. The agency of government cannot, in any sense, be deemed a party to the contract.

Third of these truths: the foregoing facts compel people to distinguish between the kinds of values they are dealing with in their exchange relations and to take such from the abstractness of value into the concrete and measure their exchange values through the use of their labor antecedents as credit values. The reason for this is that people are in contract relations with each other on an equal corporate ownership basis and are, therefore, dealing in equities of ownership.

It is no more possible to measure the relativity of values of labor and the products of labor by the use of declared value in the units of money than it is possible to calculate relative positions of celestial bodies at certain times because of a declared position of the earth by decree of a government congress, without the use of a time factor.

Fourth of these truths: the fact that the American government congress is delegated with regulatory power only in matters affecting the people's civil liberties or corporate rights and by permitting the Congress to substitute therefore the use of plenary power to declare the value of the units of the people's money (as is also the case with all other governments throughout the world) precludes any possibility of instituting a monetary system as a complement of and made a part of the people's system of private ownership—which will permit them to measure the relativity of the value of labor to the products of labor.

Since the regulation of the value of money should constitute the terms of the contract between the sovereign owners of the land of the United States of America and the private holders of said land, the units of the monetary system cannot have a fixed declared value but must be regulated in a manner that will permit the use of same by the people to declare relative credit values of labor to the products of labor, thereby giving to society a monetary system the units of which represent the relativity of all credit values.

In this manner alone can society maintain itself as self-governed by the use of regulatory laws and, by such, extend the franchise of liberty to future generations.

Fifth of these truths: the fact that the American government congress has no other alternative than to coin money, regulate the value thereof, as a unit measure of credit, is, in effect, a bar to its declaring value in the units thereof. Therefore, money can not be circulated against a debt.

If money is circulated as a credit rate measurement, it can not be circulated as a value measurement and debited in a property or properties, the corporate owners of which are of ever-changing personnel, thereby binding posterity to a fixed debt in money.

Sixth of these truths: because of the ever-changing personnel of the corporate owners of all land and the products thereof, the society living at any given time is powerless to confer, or cause to be conferred, through its agency of government, title to geographically defined units of land in perpetuity, except and only as a conditional ownership made subject to the corporate bylaws, in order to complete the people's system of private ownership, because private ownership of land and money constitute the facilities through which the benefits of corporate equities are adjusted.

A study of the six stated principles and their application, under a contract form of government, would resolve the processes of government to a simplified method compared to the complexity of present procedure, because the principles as set forth and applied through a contract are easy to understand.

(1) recognition of man's equality in his sovereign right.
(2) recognition of man's sovereign right to (socioeconomic) contract and to apply the principle of equality in that contract.
(3) separation of exchange values and utility values; thereby exchange values are taken from the abstract and are used as concrete potential values.
(4) application of these potential values to labor and the products of labor provides the method of reducing same to their credit values through the use of corporate bylaws, the units of which are used to express relativity of all credit values.
(5) and (6) are self-explanatory.

In analyzing the rights of a sovereign people and limitations involved to enter into contractual relations for the purpose of instituting government, many facts are revealed that are otherwise not apparent and which are disregarded in the interpretations made of the delegations of powers contained in the American Constitution.

First, the rights and ownership of sovereignty were recognized as the qualifying factor of each individual to enter into contractual relations.

Second, each individual was a holder of an undefined equity in all land contained within the jurisdiction of the United States.

Third, since contract relations were entered into on the

basis of equality of man's creation, and the qualifying factor of such was man's equality in his rights and ownership of sovereignty, then the equality of the rights of posterity cannot be disregarded; this leaves the people with inalienable sovereignty.

Fourth, since the purpose of organization is to restrict individual action, then upon entering into contractual relations, their sovereign equities of ownership were reduced to the status of that existing in a corporate body.

Fifth, the institution of a system of private ownership to defined units of land in perpetuity can be made only, subject to the equity rights of each member of the corporate body, to the products of the land.

Sixth, since the people's sovereign ownership is inalienable, power cannot be conferred upon a government congress to declare or fix the value of money, thereby denying to society the right to use their money for any other form of measurement.

Seventh, to ignore these facts in the interpretation of the delegation of power and to proceed to organize government in any other manner is usurpation of power, and where such is done the people of any society are governed through the police power of the state in its civil rights and in its economy. This is, therefore, autocracy.

Eighth, where organization of government is made, conforming with the foregoing stated facts, the people of a society are governed through the bylaws of its corporation in their economy and in their civil rights. This is, therefore, true democracy.

Ninth, insofar as the people's economy and their civil rights are concerned, the Congress of the United States of America is the executive board of the American people's corporation and has no discretionary power over their economy or their civil rights; in these the people of the United States are sovereign.

To those who may hold to the belief that the sovereign

power is in the people and that the agency of government is only the custodian of their sovereign power—while subscribing to the theory that the government congress has discretionary, and therefore, sovereign power to regulate the factors of the people's economy in a manner of its own choosing—they are indeed ingenious in their subtle self-deception, albeit unintentional.

Since money is the complement and is therefore a part of the people's system of private ownership of land, then the regulation of the value of money is, in effect, the regulation of private ownership of land. The method of so doing should be stated by society in its corporate bylaws. This would prevent those of the future who may be chosen to political office and who have failed to qualify themselves with an understanding of values and their implications in connection with measurements by the use of money (and whose views of society are as people to be governed) from reverting to the present procedure of declaring the value in money, thereby regaining a dictatorial power over society. Such would again restore the present monetary system with all of its attendant evils.

Regardless of the Supreme Court decisions sustaining the acts of the Congress in its interpretation of its delegated power in the regulation of the value of money, such acts must be abrogated by the people of the United States of America, who then must force Congress to regulate the value of money as a credit measurement. It is not within the prerogative of the people's agency of government to determine for itself this vital political problem, but it is rather one for the general public to decide on the policy to be instituted and made the authority by which they can reclaim unto themselves the blessings of liberty of sovereignty and to extend this franchise to all people to come.

This subject, and a logical resolution of same, is by far the most important one confronting the societies of all nations.

The important changes that would be effected by introducing the principles involved in the interpretation of the Constitution of the United States of America as a contract form of government are detailed in the following.

It would take from the president of the nation, the Congress, and the courts all discretionary power to enact and enforce legislation relative to the people's civil liberties and cause them to enact the necessary regulatory or corporate bylaws to establish the economic system as their method of self-government. This would break the bondage that enslaves people to the traditions of the past, establish them politically in keeping with the modern technological age, and give the people a system of distribution that would meet any emergency.

That certain adjustments will take place, relative to corporate operations in the fields of banking, insurance, commodity-chain merchandisers, and other large distributing organizations and that there will be an effect on interlocking directorates of milling, packing, canning, processing, and other large production facilities, together with transportation, communications, and the accumulations of vast wealth in private ownership, are inevitable, once the members of society understand their corporate rights under contract government.

To surrender present procedure in government, with its attendant advantages to some, a deterrent by far to the great mass of society, is a small price for society to pay in exchange for security. This can be more fully appreciated when weighed against the irresponsible activities of the personnel of government bodies, who, because of incompetence, are unable to furnish the people with a system of distribution capable of caring for the needs of all of society and who, therefore, directly or indirectly, keep society in a turmoil and contribute to the causes of wars between nations.

The economic system will dispose of present mythical democracy, the present concept of which is based upon the people's privilege to elect the personnel of branches for the purpose of using discretionary, therefore dictatorial, power over the people.

To continue to support a system of government founded on the precepts that forefathers surrendered their and posterity's sovereign rights to an agency borders on the ridiculous. Government, by this concept, is government by the police power of the state and is not related to true democracy, because true democracy can exist only where the inalienable sovereignty of the people is recognized and instituted under the regulatory laws proposed herein.

Those who believe that by some form of dictatorial government a more equitable distribution of wealth of a nation can be caused, whether such government exists in the form of a hereditary monarchy or whether it exists by having been seized by force of arms and the subjects thereof have been promised an equal distribution of wealth through some political method based upon socialist philosophy of economics, should first consider that any form of dictatorial government upon the death of the original leading dictatorial head must forego the uncertainties of the ability of his successor to hold the people in politico-economic subjection. Sooner or later the people will be confronted with the uncertainties caused by dissatisfaction owing to illogical discriminations on the part of the governing class, who are just as susceptible to corruption—political and economic—as the personnel of any other type of governing body.

Since the Constitution of the United States of America is a continuous contract, it is the people's heritage, and if the people of the present choose to recognize the inalienable sovereignty of man and to demand that exchange values be separated from utility values in the regulation of the value of money, thereby causing money to circulate without a debt, it is their right to demand change. As stated before in this treatise, this is the greatest political problem confronting mankind in all nations. It is not within the prerogative of people's agency of government to make this decision for them; but rather, it is one for the people of all nations to decide for themselves.

No agency of government has taken voluntary steps to correct this fundamental error of its interpretation of its delegated powers, and it is reasonable to conclude that they will take no such steps, except and only on demand of the people.

Political isms, based upon socialist philosophy, are fast making inroads upon the political convictions of many people in all nations. To counter these isms and to retain a system of government with private initiative and free enterprise, wherein said free enterprise does not encroach upon the rights of others, it is far better that people institute a monetary system wherein the units of said system reflect the relativity of all credit values, as distinct from utility values, and regulate the same in a manner that will carry out people's economic contractual relations in a logical manner. Otherwise, as in the case of the United States of America and other countries with roughly similar constitutional governments, they will lose their private initiative and free enterprise, because the present interpretation of the delegated powers in their governments, and the exercise of same, are incapable of giving people a system of distribution equal to that promised by socialism.

Attention is called once again to the inalienable sovereignty of peoples as a premise for the reasoning presented herein. This premise follows in sequence to the principles claimed as self-evident of the equality of man's creation.

On entering into a continuous contract relation, involving the people to come, the only qualification possible for the equality of creation is that all men are created equal in their rights and ownership of sovereignty. Then the people's inalienable sovereignty, and any portion thereof, cannot be delegated to an agency.

This is an entirely new concept of man's rights, relative to the power of government, and no person should ever admit his or posterity's inferiority of creation in order to confer dictatorial powers upon government, because such is not necessary to establish sound government.

In support of the foregoing premise, which makes possible the establishment of sound government in which people's inalienable sovereignty is recognized, the present accepted conclusion of value and its regulation is discarded in its entirety and is substituted by a breaking up of the abstractness of values and by using therefrom the only values used in people's exchange relations and measured by the use of money, in order to regulate people in self-government, as is their corporate right.

Dealing in the very fundamentals of human rights and sovereign ownerships by use of a corporate form of government, wherein any society is governed by its corporate bylaws, in effect gives people true democracy and is the surest way to combat the illogic of autocratic government.

To convince one as to the soundness of these postulates, the test is simple and infallible: Was the generation who adopted the Constitution of the United States of America as the authority for government possessed with a superior power over the generations to follow, in that they could sign the sovereign rights of posterity away and delegate such irrevocably to the agency they created for government?

If present people's decision of the foregoing is negative, then they must admit that society has the right to establish itself under a corporate form of government by use of exchange values as distinguished from utility values, defined in this treatise, and circulate both money and commodities as the credit evidences of labor performed, in order that the values of labor and the products of labor can be made to balance, through the use of the regulatory laws set forth in this treatise.

The very purpose of the organization of the corporate or

constitutional form of government is to give people equal equity-holding in a corporate form of government and, therefrom, economic security from the beginning to the end of their life cycles.

Thus can end the tyranny of laws enacted at the discretion of legislative bodies and sustained by the political convictions of the personnel of courts of law.